BREAKING POINT

BREAKING POINT

The College Affordability Crisis and Our Next Financial Bubble

Kevin W. Connell

ROWMAN & LITTLEFIELD
Lanham • Boulder • New York • London

Published by Rowman & Littlefield
A wholly owned subsidary of The Rowman & Littlefield Publishing Group,
Inc.
4501 Forbes Boulevard, Suite 200, Lanham, Maryland 20706
www.rowman.com

Unit A, Whitacre Mews, 26-34 Stannary Street, London SE11 4AB

British Library Cataloguing in Publication Information Available

Library of Congress Cataloging-in-Publication Data

Names: Connell, Kevin, 1992- author.
Title: Breaking point : the college affordability crisis and our next financial bubble / Kevin W.
    Connell.
Description: Lanham : Rowman & Littlefield, [2016] | Includes bibliographical references.
Identifiers: LCCN 2016019223 (print) | LCCN 2016032004 (ebook) | ISBN 9781475826029
    (cloth : alk. paper) | ISBN 9781475826036 (pbk. : alk. paper) | ISBN 9781475826043 (Elec-
    tronic)
Subjects: LCSH: College costs--United States. | United States--Economic conditions--21st centu-
    ry.
Classification: LCC LB2342 .C6647 2016 (print) | LCC LB2342 (ebook) | DDC 378.3/8--dc23
LC record available at https://lccn.loc.gov/2016019223

∞ ™ The paper used in this publication meets the minimum requirements of
American National Standard for Information Sciences—Permanence of Paper
for Printed Library Materials, ANSI/NISO Z39.48-1992.

Printed in the United States of America

For my mentor, Thomas H. Jackson

CONTENTS

ACKNOWLEDGMENTS

This book is a culmination of attempts to make sense of the financial conundrum within higher education. As a college student, the research I have completed is particularly important to me because I am living it as a reality. Plaguing the hearts and minds of average Americans across the country, households are becoming progressively buried under a mountain of national student loan debt that has accrued to over $1.3 trillion, which continues to grow with every passing year.

This book will achieve its goal if it prods scholars and ordinary people alike to discuss this crisis that is upon us. The hope is that this discussion will develop to the point of provoking debate among legislators on Capitol Hill, encouraging them to act. If ignored, the financial debacle of the student loan crisis will mushroom into an economic calamity, most certainly larger than that of the mortgage crisis in 2008.

Much of this project relies on the past work of others, and it is their thoughts that have assisted and inspired me to contribute to the discussion. Continually building upon this movement of growing concern, I am confident that this work can add to and encourage the dialogue that has occurred and continues to be had.

This book owes a great deal to many people, starting with the teachers at Rush-Henrietta Central School District. Growing up, my teachers instilled in me a love and skill for learning, and while each of them had a uniquely lasting impact on my life, Mr. Ross Amstey deserves special recognition in this regard. As my AP Language and Composition teacher at Rush-Henrietta High School, Mr. Amstey was the first educator to have a significant impact on my writing. Only after establishing a strong foundation of critical thinking and rhetorical writing skills under his care did I have the capacity to write something of this scope. More importantly, Mr. Amstey instilled in me a love for the art of writing and rhetoric, a gift that will remain with me for the rest of my life.

During the same time I was writing this book, several professors had a profound impact me as both a scholar and a person. Professors Gerald Gamm, Bill Tiberio, and Curt Smith are among the most influential instructors that I credit for molding me into the devoted scholar and person I have become. Each of them has challenged me throughout my college experience and provided me with a solid foundation of knowledge in the area of political studies. However, more important than anything else, they have served as personal role models whom I consider to be three of the most compassionate and decent people I have ever had the good fortune of knowing.

In regard to my research, two people deserve particular praise for their efforts that started me down the right and necessary path of penning this work. In respect to the material on colleges raising tuition, Professor Ronald G. Ehrenberg, Irving M. Ives Professor of Industrial and Labor Relations and Economics at Cornell University, Stephen H. Weiss Presidential Fellow, and director of the Cornell Higher Education Research Institute, discussed his perspective on the subject on multiple occasions and directed me to sources that were an invaluable asset to chapters 2 and 3.

As for my work concerning Sallie Mae, Professor Thomas Stanton, fellow at the Center for Advanced Governmental Studies at Johns Hopkins University and former director of the FTC Office of Policy Planning under President Clinton, deserves a great deal of recognition as well. Not only have several of his published works assisted me in the daunting task of fully understanding the operations and evolution of Sallie Mae, but he also devoted his own personal time to correspond with me in grappling over the complex nature of the student lending system.

My family has also played an instrumental role in helping me through this grueling process. My aunt and uncle, Julianne and Paul Jordan, as well as my late grandmother, Marie Hanes, have all been a source of support for the growth and direction of the book. My Aunt Julie in particular helped me throughout the final stages of the editing process, making the transition to publication possible. Finally, my grandfather, Leo Hanes, deserves special recognition in this regard. There were many times when I called him late at night for guidance and reassurance. Had he not been there to listen and offer words of encouragement, the writing process would have been nearly impossible to overcome.

Many friends have also gone to extraordinary efforts to help me through this process in a number of ways. Alex Yudelson, Zack Hilt, Adam Hotchkiss, Robert Marks, Greg Bischoping, Jared Jones, Brian Kos, Vincent Lawyer, Joseph Henderson, Tad Mack, Ben Stilson, Joe Morelle, Harry Bronson, Dan Gorman, Chris Fallon, Nannette Nocon, Evan Dawson, Cody Combs, Bob Newman, Bob and Colleen Regelsberger, Mark Lenzi, Paul McAndrews, Rafael E. Báez, Jake Sweely, Alexis Wallace, Jon Aho, Joseph Glick, and Myles Mack-Mercer were continuing sources of support and inspiration who helped see this project through to the end.

There are two individuals who stand out as having had the most profound impact on me to date. The first person, who has influenced me more than any other person in this world, is my mother. Her life-long devotion to a career in primary education, steadfast determination to overcome adversity, and relentless love and support for me since the day I was born have all worked to collectively influence and sustain me more than any other person. Had it not been for her, I would not be equipped with the skills and character necessary to see this task through to the end.

Finally, the most deserving person of acknowledgment, who was most directly associated with this project, is Professor Thomas H. Jackson, president emeritus of the University of Rochester, whom I have had the esteemed honor of working with throughout my entire college journey. Not only has he been instrumental in offering valuable insight and assistance throughout this process, but he also instilled in me the invaluable blessing of humility in its finest form. Without his guidance and inspiration, not only would this book fail to exist, but I would not be the person I am today. For these reasons, I gladly dedicate this work to him.

FOREWORD

In 2003, I sent my daughter off to college and through that experience I learned firsthand how difficult it is to navigate the college process on your own. To my dismay, I read at that time there was over $200 billion in outstanding college debt. With many of my friends and acquaintances struggling with the same issue of financing a college education for their children, I saw an opportunity as an entrepreneur to help parents and students get through this confusing process and started a college consulting business. My goal was to help parents and students graduate on time with less stress, less disruption, and less debt. Although it has been a very fulfilling and rewarding business helping families through the college process, it has also proven to be discouraging as the problem continues to get worse.

Breaking Point: The College Affordability Crisis and Our Next Financial Bubble reveals the rich history on how college began and why for years it has helped many people achieve amazing things that, without a higher education, might never have accomplished. Unfortunately, as *Breaking Point* highlights, there is also a dark side to the big picture. Shedding light on this important and often overshadowed problem, *Breaking Point* specifically points to the reasons causing the recent surge in higher education costs and offers bold policy proposals to implement the changes necessary to avoid another economic crisis.

Many of the issues raised in *Breaking Point* are ones that I have encountered over the years presenting to and meeting with thousands of families. The one thing that has been consistent with almost all the families planning for higher education is that very few of them have saved enough for college, and it is no wonder why. Over the last 35 years, inflation adjusted college costs have surged by over 1100 percent. This rate far outstrips medical, energy, and food costs over that same period of time. Because the government has gotten involved with giving students and parents the ability to borrow non-secured money to pay for college, many families borrow vast sums of money with the hope of securing a good job after graduation. Over time, this borrowing has accrued to a national student loan debt of 1.6 trillion dollars.

The disturbing news about borrowing all this money is that many students who are graduating with college degrees cannot find a job in their field. The statistics are startling when we hear that 50 percent of students graduating are either unemployed or in jobs that do not require a college degree. Combined with all the inefficiencies in the system, this point alone should make a parent step back and really think about the value of the degree their child is earning. Many of the degrees colleges offer are called "soft," meaning that they add very little practical value in the marketplace and students consequently find it very difficult to get a job in that field. Thus, it is critical that parents and students learn the value of different fields in the marketplace as they prepare to enroll in academic programs so they leave college with a degree that will provide them the best opportunity of a career when they graduate. Otherwise, they could face the very real reality of leaving college with a huge debt and no tangible way of paying it off. The consequence of this regular situation is one where graduates, now stripped of their purchasing power, are forced to forego major financial and life decisions, such as buying a car, purchasing a home, saving for retirement, or getting married and starting a family.

On a related point of being competitive in the job market upon graduation, it is also very important to get some exposure with different careers before choosing a major. That means talking to and shadowing people in the field you are interested in. I say this because the average student changes majors four times. This not only is disruptive, but it is why the average student takes five-and-a-half years to graduate with a bachelor's degree. Parents and students need to understand that college is a BIG business and they do not care how long you stay in college. In fact, the longer you stay enrolled in school, the more money the colleges and lenders collect. This is arguably one of many reasons that colleges make their facilities so luxurious, as *Breaking Point* discusses in great detail. The fitness centers, dorms, academic buildings, dining halls, and about everything else imaginable is being built first class. When faced with the decision of continuing on in the country club atmosphere or facing the reality of underemployment and poverty, it is understandable why many students choose the former over the latter. Along with all these inefficiencies, one out of three students drop out or transfer in the first two years and unfortunately many have student loan debt.

If you are one of the 66 percent of parents who wonders if a college education is going to pay off, you are not alone. It is very important to look at this from a serious financial perspective and calculate if the ROI is really worth it. I know from meeting with families it is hard not to want to give the best for your children. However, giving into the emotions of sending your child to the college "of their choice" only to possibly be saddled with debt for 10–20 years is often not what is best for them in the long run. Borrowing from 401K retirement savings and taking out home equity lines of credit can often lead to long term financial hardship and huge amounts of stress as well. When we think about the over 150,000 parents that are having their social security garnished because of student loans, we begin to understand that the college debt crisis is not the paranoia of pundits detached from reality, but it is a very real hardship facing families across America every day.

With many companies in the modern economy demanding that applicants have a college education even to be considered for a career puts tremendous pressure on people contemplating whether to attend to college. We have consistently heard the statistics that a person with a college education makes much more income over their lifetime than those without a college degree. Nonetheless, people must also weigh the debt burden that needs to be paid to receive a college education and lost opportunity cost of not working for 4–5 years while attending college. Ultimately, the decision to attend college requires much more thought than it did 20 or 30 years ago, and with time it is only becoming harder to make that determination. Although practical programs at community colleges and vocational schools continue to be stigmatized, these programs are becoming more attractive as an alternative to vast sums of debt for liberal arts degrees at four-year institutions that are proving to diminish in value as time goes on.

If readers take anything away from this book, it should be the following. College is a BIG business, no different than any other at their core, and their primary goal is to recruit the best students they can, fill all the seats, and generate revenue. They are the best marketing machine out there that data mines all the information they can about you to increase their chances of having you attend their college. While college used to be a simple investment in a brighter future, modern trends suggest that the decision to attend college is becoming increasingly more difficult and the growing national student debt poses a serious threat as this problem persists. If nothing else, remember that pursuing a college education is one of the top three financial decisions a person will make in their lifetime. When you understand these simple points, it should drive you to become a more educated parent and student before making a decision and *Breaking Point* will help you to that end. Enjoy the book!

—Phil James, CCO, Chief College Officer, CAP Advisory Services, Inc.

INTRODUCTION

The Ticking Time Bomb

There was a time when a college degree was reasonably affordable to the everyday consumer. These relatively inexpensive degrees were also reliable in virtually guaranteeing a well-paying job upon graduation. Consequently, the generations of my parents and grandparents left college with degrees valued by the job market for a reasonable cost.

The current generation of young men and women, however, face a far different scenario. As William J. Bennett, former U.S. Secretary of Education, has said, "A college degree was once synonymous with academic excellence and workforce readiness. Today, it seems synonymous with debt and underemployment."[1] Since 1966, college tuition and fees have surged by approximately 1,580 percent at four-year private colleges, 2,050 percent at four-year out-of-state public colleges, and 2,720 percent at four-year in-state public colleges.[2]

The inevitable result of this rise in college costs is an astounding national student loan debt that suffocates households under massive financial burdens. At over $1.3 trillion, student loan debt has eclipsed credit card debt for the first time in American history.[3]

To make this figure more tangible in terms of understanding how it impacts families, the Pew Research Center reported that a record one in five households held student loan debt at an average of $23,000 in 2011,[4] which has now jumped to over $35,000 in 2015.[5] However, the micro- and macro-economic impact of this debt has not emerged within

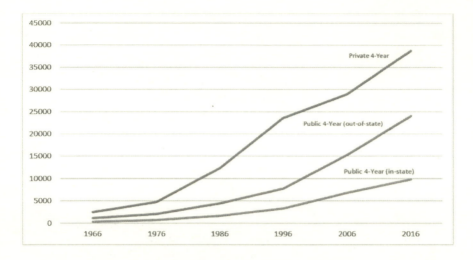

Figure 0.1.   Cost of Attendance since 1966 (in Current Dollars).   Source: Nation-
*al Center for Education Statistics, "Table 320: Average Undergraduate Tuition and Fees
and Room and Board Rates Charged for Full-Time Students in Degree-Granting Institutions, by Type and Control of Institution: 1964–65 through 2006–07," U.S. Department
of Education Institute of Education Sciences, 2008, https://nces.ed.gov/programs/digest/
d07/tables/dt07_320.asp (accessed February 20, 2016); Travis Mitchell, "See 20 Years of
Tuition Growth at National Universities," U.S. News & World Report, July 29, 2015,
www.usnews.com/education/best-colleges/paying-for-college/articles/2015/07/29/
chart-see-20-years-of-tuition-growth-at-national-universities (accessed February 20,
2016).*

a vacuum—rather, its implications have had a broad ripple effect
throughout the entire American economy.

One of the most disturbing consequences of national college debt is
that many people are now forced to put off other purchases that are
essential to the health of our economy, such as investing in a car or a
home or saving for retirement. Young men and women are also increasingly compelled to move back in with their parents, prolonging the
delay in starting their adult lives, starting families, and so on. Moreover,
many parents of college students are also taking on even greater debt
burdens with large PLUS loans, which frequently cause people to forego retiring at a reasonable age just so they can afford to pay for their
contribution to their child's college education.

This is occurring at the same time that a college degree is widely
considered to be a necessary investment in ensuring a decent standard
of living. If the price of higher education is not reduced, some speculate

that the American dream will be reduced to nothing more than a memory of the past.

Reflecting on the direction that higher education financing has taken since the 1960s, we must consider possible reasons that have led up to the unprecedented surge in its cost that we see today. I understand the causes of the explosion in college debt to be threefold: (1) the objective of prestige-seeking on behalf of colleges and universities, (2) short-sighted demand in amenities and a blind faith in the college system on behalf of students, and (3) predatory lending on behalf of large college debt lenders, both private and public.

We first explore the priorities of these associated groups, which have systematically undermined the mission for college affordability, and exactly how each has contributed to the exponential surge in higher education costs over the last several decades. From there, we investigate several proposals, with the purpose of creating a higher education market that is sustainable.

These proposals are made with serious consideration of their implications, but out of calculated necessity before it is too late to avoid another economic crisis, which appears inevitable if the status quo remains on its present course.

Before venturing into the specific components of each section, it is important to begin by reflecting upon a question that is at the core of this entire discussion: *What is the purpose of higher education?*

As I will explain later in greater detail, college was largely limited to the wealthy until the mid-twentieth century. However, with the Soviet Union emerging as a preeminent economic and military power in an ever-growing global economy, the United States began to subsidize the cost of attending college to give the masses the opportunity to think and innovate with a college education.

With the GI Bill (1944), National Defense Education Act (1958), and Higher Education Act (1965), Congress laid the foundation for educating large amounts of the population with the intended purpose of creating a stronger and more technologically developed economy throughout the Cold War.

Speaking to this point, Suzanne Mettler comments in her book, *Degrees of Inequality*, that this surge of financial support for institutions of higher education "expanded access to college to growing numbers of Americans from across the income spectrum," enabling people from modest backgrounds "to enjoy occupational choices and a standard of living their parents could only have dreamed of."[6]

Over the course of the last several decades, however, institutions of all kinds have deviated from this simple investment, arguably wasting billions of dollars in federal and state subsidies that are generated by taxpayer revenue each year. Rather than limiting programs to those that will help the individual and society alike, colleges at every level have ushered in a new era of enabling huge numbers of students to study virtually whatever they want, no matter how minimal the return is to the individual student or society upon graduation.

Consequently, higher education has converted from a system that "facilitates upward mobility" to one that "now engenders the creation of something that increasingly resembles a caste system," widening social and economic divisions.[7] Although the job market is under a constant state of evolution, every sector has a limit on the amount of people it needs to supply that particular field. Under the status quo, colleges of all types ignore job market demand, often continuing to expand programs that are related to fields that are either fixed or even diminishing in size relative to job market demand.

Take a field that is even growing and undersupplied, such as healthcare—say a room of one hundred people represents the national enrollment in higher education. If only a single person of these one hundred people studies medicine, that person is going to be very well off. However, as more and more people study medicine and enter that particular field, the market eventually reaches a saturation point. At that point, it is no longer a sound investment to study in that field, because an imbalance in the ratio of supply and demand has caused the tangible worth of the degree to diminish significantly in its return.

In other words, we should not have each of those one hundred students attend medical school, because our society does not require every single person to be a doctor. Building upon this premise, we can begin to question the recent trend of political leaders calling for every single American to attend college and pursue a traditional liberal arts degree. Although it would be wonderful if we could send everyone to a four-year liberal arts institution, the unfortunate reality is that the job market simply does not demand such a model.

Attempting to enroll every single person in the United States into a four-year liberal arts program at a premium price, no matter how admirable in thought, not only fails to promote the demands from society and the job market, but also does a grave disservice to both the students and collective body of taxpayers alike.

Not only is tax revenue squandered on educating students in fields with minimal employment demand, but the students also often find themselves buried under large amounts of debt with little to no better prospect of employment because of the skill set associated with their degree. Dubbing the status quo as a "college-for-all crusade," *Washington Post* columnist Robert Samuelson wrote, "We overdid it. The obsessive faith in college has backfired."[8]

Although there is the argument that a liberal arts degree serves more of a purpose than as a pathway to employment, the primary focus of any degree must be to promote the financial security of both the individual and the society that helped subsidize his or her education. It makes little sense to spend tens or even hundreds of thousands of dollars and years of time to simply learn how to think better without improving employment prospects or earnings potential, much less one's ability to apply those skills in a career or the world around them.

If improved insight and thought on the world does not lead to self-advancement and production in society that will subsidize the next generation of students, then what is the point of the new knowledge when it cannot even be applied in a practical sense? While this certainly is not the only focus of this book, these are some important thoughts to keep in mind as we continue our discussion on both what is causing the college affordability crisis and how we can move forward to fix it before this ticking time bomb erupts.

I

SOWING THE SEEDS OF CRISIS

Higher education in America has not always been what it is today. Over the course of our nation's history, education has evolved as much in its purpose and access as it has in value and price. Today, higher education in the United States has a number of salient characteristics. These include, but are not limited to, the scope and average size of its institutions; the coexistence of small liberal arts colleges and large research universities; the large share of enrollment in the public sector; the widespread funding on behalf of states to operate these public institutions; and the professional schools woven into the fabric of universities.

Our modern system of higher education is the product of a four-hundred-year-old evolution. What we have defined as higher learning has changed dramatically in both size and subject over the course of this evolution. However, the single largest differentiating factor between colleges and universities of early America and the institutions of today is that while the latter lacks a precise focus, the former did not. In the words of the esteemed American scholar Frederick Rudolph, "At the beginning, higher education in America would be governed less by accident than by certain purpose, less by impulse than by design."[1] During our long and hard-fought journey toward modernization and progress, we simply lost our way.

In the beginning, the early purpose and design of American higher education was parochial. Harvard, for example, was established in 1636 by the Puritans, acknowledging their responsibility to create stabilizing institutions for the future. The "cardinal principles" of English Puritan-ism rested upon the development of two significant classes: "a learned clergy, and a lettered people."[2] Harvard, among other institutions, was established in essence to create the "competent rulers" who would lead future generations.[3]

While most of the early American colleges and universities were united in their mission to promote religion, much of the development and growth of these institutions stemmed from competition between denominations. In a religious turf war, the Puritans of New England at Harvard and Yale were competing for influence against the Presbyter-ians of the Middle Colonies, as one example, who later established Princeton University in 1746.

Although most institutions in early American higher education were parochial-centered, the splintering of existing religions into new de-nominations during the Great Awakening shattered the pattern of state-church colleges that had dominated American higher education for over a century. "The rivalry and diversity inspired by the Great Awaken-ing created colleges in which the strength of religious ties varied, and by the end of the colonial period diversity and toleration had become values of such importance," that by the early nineteenth century, most colleges "claimed only incidental interest in religion or only a loosely acknowledged denominational connection."[4]

In the void of religion, many colleges adopted a new mission of helping to form and sustain the creation of a new system of government during the revolutionary period. In essence, the focus of higher educa-tion transitioned from creating church leaders to political leaders. William and Mary, for example, embraced a mission as a school of civil service training that would produce appointed surveyors, county clerks, and clerks to the colonial government.[5]

Although this transition from training parochial leaders to public servants was successful, "the colonial college failed to establish itself as a popular institution intimately affecting the lives of the people."[6] Col-leges remained, by and large, as institutions accessible only to the wealthy, "where, for want of suitable Genius they learn[ed] little more than to carry themselves handsomely, and enter a Room genteely."[7] While colleges and universities are perceived by many today to be an agent of social mobility with widespread access, colleges and universities during the colonial period helped to solidify rigid class structures with both the cost as well as the curriculum.

"The costs required available cash, something which many people of middling and lower class did not have."[8] Additional costs included the geographic barriers as well. "When the College of New Jersey opened its doors in 1746, it was the only college between Williamsburg and New Haven. Most American farmers—and most Americans *were* farmers—could not afford to give up their sons' labor, their sons' help at home."[9]

Aside from the costs, "the curriculum was not of the sort that appealed to men of practical inclination," thus limiting the benefits of a higher education only to those with the luxury and privilege to forego the need to develop a practical trade.[10]

Despite the transition from parochial to civil training during the colonial and revolutionary eras, the cost and content of the curriculum made college an expensive and unnecessary commodity for most Americans. "The college had long been a necessity for society, but it had not become a necessity for the people. . . . For most colonial Americans, college was something that could wait."[11]

In the aftermath of the Revolutionary War, the United States underwent a shift in both access and purpose for higher education. "The Revolution damaged buildings, enrollments, endowments and reputations, but far more fundamental was the damage done to the old purposes and to the old course of study."[12] Caught in the new wave of democratic spirit, and sensitive to the importance of the common man, nineteen colleges were chartered between 1782 and 1802, "more than twice as many colleges as had been founded during the almost 150 years previous."[13]

With this new influx of colleges, spurred by denominational rivalry, expanding religious toleration, state loyalty, increasing wealth, and a growing population, colleges began offering a broader appeal to middle class Americans, recognizing that colleges could be used as a way to advance in society. State legislatures, understanding the significance of this transition, began taking a more active role in higher education. The North Carolina state legislature, for example, adopted a resolution, stating that "all useful learning shall be duly encouraged and promoted in one or more universities."[14]

Securing an increasing investment on behalf of the government, colleges and universities were encouraged to adopt more practical curriculum that would expand the benefits of a college degree from the small social circles of the elite to create an educated class that would benefit the nation as a whole.

At William and Mary, Thomas Jefferson proposed to "establish a professorship of anatomy, medicine, and chemistry, revealing as he did so the new emphasis on utility which would characterize the American college curriculum."[15] George Washington even expected the advent of a National University that would be directed as a tool to shape "a class of men free from the restricting prejudices of provincialism and sectionalism. . . . The plans spoke much of science, of preparation for democratic citizenship, of escaping from the past."[16]

Continuing to build upon the transition toward the idea of an "American University" that would serve more than just as a finishing school for the sons of wealthy gentlemen, an unprecedented surge of growth in colleges swept the nation. "The American people went into the American Revolution with nine colleges. They went into the Civil War with approximately 250."[17] In 1837, Phillip Lindsley, president of the University of Nashville, concluded that "our busy, restless, speculating, moneymaking people" required colleges to be as scattered and mobile as the American people themselves.[18]

Colleges, in many ways, emerged during this period as the product of a rapidly expanding and modernizing society during the Industrial Revolution of the nineteenth century. "College-founding in the nineteenth century was undertaken in the same spirit as canal-building, cotton-ginning, farming, and gold-mining. All were touched by the American faith in tomorrow, in the unquestionable capacity of Americans to achieve a better world . . . and endless progress."[19]

Part of Henry Clay's *American System*, colleges would be the epicenters of intellect and innovation. The American University, in other words, would be the engine room capable of propelling the United States into the international arena as a modern industrialized power.

As America modernized, the spirit of the Revolutionary Period continued to grow well into the nineteenth century. "In America, democracy's pervasive influence was to inspire a system of education reflecting the values of the republican form of government that had been invented after the Revolution."[20] As Lawrence A. Cremin observed, the new

American education was to be "purged of all vestiges of older monarchial forms and dedicated to the creation of a cohesive and independent citizenry."[21]

Associated increasingly with the benefits of an active citizenry, educational initiatives starting in the 1820s were intended to prop up a practical and useful education that appealed to the common people. This idea of expanding American higher education for practical use, however, was part of something larger. American democracy itself was an expanding proposition, in that the whole of America was expanding access to opportunity and luxury to the masses.

> By 1828, on the eve of Andrew Jackson's election as President, universal male suffrage had been achieved in all states north of Virginia save Rhode Island. Voting rights were in most cases secured merely by establishing residence in a community and showing some means of financial support. The development held ramifications for American education: the franchise had been extended to all adult white males . . . thus empowered, the electorate could have some influence on the course of public education.[22]

Spearheaded by Jacksonian Democracy and the "age of the common man," the movement to democratize higher education was more specifically a "protest of labor groups against the prevailing order and a significant movement in the unleashing of American capitalism," both of which harbored "a fundamental hostility to privilege."[23] Creating pressure in educational and political spheres to extend education to the industrial classes, an emphasis was shifted away from "the elitist enterprise" of the classic higher education model, prompting the "emergence of smaller, private colleges" that aligned with the needs of industry.

Although some private nonprofit universities embraced this model, for-profit colleges emerged as the primary enterprise to satisfy this demand. For example, a large-scale network of Bartlett schools was founded by R. Montgomery Bartlett in Philadelphia, Pittsburgh, and Cincinnati between 1834 and 1838. Marked by "the establishment of the early business colleges by individual entrepreneurs," this wave of for-profit colleges during the Jacksonian Era mastered the art of combining penmanship, arithmetic, and bookkeeping into one institution, establishing a "basic curriculum" upon which the new labor force of the modern masses was to be trained.[24]

Whether through traditional nonprofit institutions or the emerging class of entrepreneurial for-profit colleges, the purpose and demand of the new curriculum were one and the same. "The eastern workingman who sought a larger share of the results of his own labor, who asked for a shorter working week that he might enjoy the benefits of freedom" signified that the masses were ready to adopt a more modern and inclusive economy.[25] However, it was far more than that.

> It went beyond the agrarianism of Jefferson and recognized the development of manufacturing as an American interest; it saw beyond Jefferson's yeoman farmer to the creation of a more complex class structure, one that encompassed men of property and men of labor as well. It committed itself so fully to the Jeffersonian faith in the people that all of Jefferson's fine distinctions, all of his careful reliance on an aristocracy of talent, all of his wise reservation on human capacities were abandoned in heady embrace of the people.[26]

In other words, higher education was evolving in an atmosphere of expanding suffrage and an unlimited belief in material and moral progress. However, as it turns out, several factors would keep traditional higher education institutions from taking the lead in the movement for social mobility of the industrial class under Jacksonian Democracy. This was largely the case because "common" primary schools and for-profit colleges would instead lead the movement.

First, Jacksonians practically emphasized that primary or "common" school would be both necessary and sufficient for providing the type of education that would satisfy the interests of the industrial class. "Between 1830 and 1860 the American people came to accept the idea that the provision of common schools was a public obligation."[27]

Prevailing predominantly in the North and West, Horace Mann, along with James G. Carter, Henry Barnard, and William Russell, "argued that these institutions should be publically controlled, publically supported, and open to all."[28] Emphasizing practical and moral education, Mann believed that common schools should "provide the basis for the exercise of responsible citizenship" and teach practical skills that would help elevate its pupils to the business class.[29]

Influencing American public education for more than a century, Mann's common school movement had widespread influence throughout the United States. Prior to Mann's proposals, widespread education even for children was not considered to be a role for public investment.

> On the eve of the American Revolution, except in New England, there was not public provision for elementary education in the American colonies. . . . The responsibility for education rested largely with the parents who, if they could manage a little instruction in reading, writing, and arithmetic, felt they had done well by their children, as they indeed had.[30]

However, with the advent and spreading of Mann's philosophy, education in America would begin on a journey to universalization. "By 1830, aggregate (primary and secondary, and higher) school attendance rates for whites between the ages of five and nineteen were about 35 percent. By 1860, the rates had risen to about 58 percent of the eligible population."[31]

In other words, 5.5 million of 9.5 million children between the ages of five and nineteen years old were enrolled in some level of education. Recognizing the importance of these basic skills, states began to pass compulsory primary education laws, beginning with Massachusetts in 1852 and ending with Mississippi in 1917, solidifying access to education for the whole of the industrial class.[32]

Second, the development of for-profit colleges, narrowly tailored to fit the needs of an expanding workforce and replacing the old system of apprenticeship, was able to satisfy the demands of the industrial class beyond primary school. "The 1840s and 1850s introduced the reaper, the telegraph, and the sewing machine. Patents issued by the government grew in number from 436 in 1837 to 993 in 1850, and to 4,778 in 1860."[33] With each passing year, the United States was becoming exponentially more modern and industrialized. Technology changed the workforce, which in turn redefined society. But for this to occur, the workforce needed to be trained.

In growing numbers, entrepreneurs such as Henry B. Bryant and Henry D. Stratton, students at Folsom Business College in Cleveland, continued to open colleges in the entrepreneurial spirit to satisfy the growing demand for practical job training. Forming a partnership in 1853 with James W. Lusk, a professor of Spencerian penmanship in northern Ohio, the Bryant and Stratton Mercantile College was opened in Cleveland.[34]

Building upon their initial success, Bryant and Stratton branched out to several major cities in the Northeast and Midwest, including Buffalo in 1854, Chicago in 1866, and Albany in 1867.[35] By the end of the decade, Bryant and Stratton had established colleges in forty-four locations, spanning from St. Louis to Boston. This massive expansion by Bryant and Stratton and others like it was reflected in reports filed by the U.S. Bureau of Education, which found that "from the estimated twenty [for-profit] colleges in operation in 1850, at least 250 institutions enrolling more than 81,000 students were operating in 1890."[36]

Although traditional higher education would not take the lead in the Jacksonian movement, either by accident or by design, colleges continued to emerge in greater numbers and modernize in its missions. Consequently, enrollments in liberal arts colleges "increased fourteen-fold between 1800 and 1860, from 1,156 students to 16,000. Just as significant, the percentage of young men between the ages of fifteen and twenty who chose to go to colleges increased between 200 and 250 percent."[37]

As colleges continued to expand and while the American faith in a more collectively prosperous future still prevailed, the college movement itself was not a single cooperative effort. Much like the early denominational battles between religions in colonial higher education, states competed against one another for dominance in the new order of federalist America and ultimately led to the conception of the "State College" systems that are in place today.[38]

In 1851, for example, a Minnesota newspaper encouraged the development of a state university with the assertion that "not a single youth of either sex would be permitted to leave the territory to acquire an education for want" of its own state university.[39] Colleges, in many ways, were seen as a practical investment for the state in the same way as modern transportation systems and technology. The underlying notion was that to compete in a federalist society, a state would have to make continual investments to attract new residents and dominate in the movement toward modernization. Ultimately,

"State College" became synonymous with opportunity, which was a synonym for America itself. It was an invitation to leave the farm, to join the ever-growing movement to the cities, to achieve the technical competence to build bridges, to mine the earth, to win some final mastery over time.[40]

In an effort to outcompete surrounding and rival states, "The American college was conceived of as a social investment," which ultimately worked to promote the expansion, access, and practicality of higher education across the country. [41] In the words of Joseph McKeen, the first president of Bowdoin College:

> It ought always be remembered, that literary institutions are founded and endowed for the common good, and not for the private advantage of those who resort to them for education. It is not that they may be able to pass through life in an easy or reputable manner, but that their powers may be cultivated and improved for the benefit of society. If it be true no man should live for himself alone, we may safely assert that every man who has been aided by a public institution to acquire an education and to qualify himself for usefulness, is under peculiar obligation to exert his talents for the public good. [42]

In other words, higher education was to be invested in by the public not for the amusement of the individual, but for the benefit of society. Ultimately, the "social purpose might also be defined as national purpose. A commitment to the republic became a guiding obligation of the American college." [43]

Despite the hopes of McKeen, a model founded on a civic obligation never came to pass. As the nature of American society changed throughout the nineteenth and twentieth centuries, so did the expectations of its colleges. So much so that "the time came when graduates discovered that a college education as a social investment was now of less importance than a college education as a personal investment." [44]

Influenced by the motives of its students, government, and the institutions themselves, traditional institutions of nonprofit higher education ultimately chose a middle way between the classical curriculum model of the colonial period and the modern vocational model of for-profit colleges. This model has come to be known as the prevailing liberal arts degree. Starting in the mid-nineteenth century, "the old-time college would change significantly and it would find itself increasingly surrounded by new institutions that were addressing themselves effectively to the question of intellectual and popular purpose to which the first two hundred and twenty-five years of American higher education had given but faltering, uncertain answers." [45]

During the same time also came advancements in the natural and physical sciences, profoundly influencing the college movement toward a model centered less in the old classics. Shaking the colleges loose of their old convictions, science would be the "great disrupter of the classical course of study" in working to strike a balance between the classical model and the vocational system.[46]

Although scientists had not achieved significant respect by the mid-nineteenth century, the work of scientific pioneers worked to popularize it. Combining the richness of the American continent in making science an instrument for exploiting the great natural wealth of inland America, these emerging fields offered broad utility that the classical studies could not possibly achieve. Minerology and mechanical engineering, for example, would fundamentally change mining operations during the latter half of the nineteenth century, replacing old surface mining techniques like panning with modern approaches like hydraulic mining.[47]

A potential explanation for this emphasis might rest in the fact that the United States, although modernizing, would not fully industrialize until decades later. "Before 1860, the nation remained overwhelmingly rural and agrarian. In 1820, only 5 percent of the population lived in cities over 8,000; by 1830, that figure had risen only slightly to 6.75 percent."[48] Even on the eve of the Civil War, "80 percent of the population fell into the so-called 'industrious classes,' composed mainly of farmers but including mechanics, artisans, laborers, and—to a degree—shopkeepers and businessmen."[49]

Although vocational schools would satisfy much of the demand for training with emerging technologies, the writing was on the wall. The dawn of a new age was on the horizon for American society, and higher education would react, slowly, once again. "The era of science still lay ahead, but the emergence of the B.S. and Ph.B. degrees and the creation of scientific departments . . . suggested that the American college was perhaps in the neighborhood of discovering some way of making a vital connection with American society."[50]

Under this "utilitarian impulse," Congress passed the Morrill Land-Grant College Act of 1862, the object of the act being

> to give a chance to the industrial classes of the country to obtain a
> liberal education, something more than what was bestowed by our

universities and colleges in general, which seemed to be more based
on the English plan of giving education only to what might be called
the professional classes, in law, medicine, and theology.

The act itself provided support for institutions "where the leading object shall be, without excluding other scientific or classical studies, to
teach such branches of learning as are related to agriculture and the
mechanic arts."[51]

Recognizing the importance of practical education in America, Congress would assist land-grant colleges in the mission to offer a practical
and well-rounded education to its students, so much so that "by the
1890s, the utilitarian impulse had permeated the university movement."[52] As David Starr Jordan of Stanford University said, "The entire
university movement is toward reality and practicality."[53]

The movement, however, would remain in the balance between the
old classical model and the purely vocational model, largely due to the
sentiments of those like Henry Phillip Tappan of the University of
Michigan. No friend of pure vocationalism, Tappan made clear before
he went to Michigan that the true university would be "a powerful
counter influence against the excessive commercial spirit, and against
the chicanery and selfishness of demagoguism."[54]

Tappan went on to say that an American university would demonstrate to a skeptical public the true meaning of scholarship. "We shall
have no more acute distinctions drawn between scholastic and practical
education; for, it will be seen that all true education is practical, and
that practice without education is little worth; and then there will be
dignity, grace, and a resistless charm about scholarship and the scholar."[55]

Others were not, however, sold on the idea that scholastic and practical education were inseparable. John William Draper, a professor at
New York University, suggested, "To what are the great advances of
civilization for the last fifty years due—to literature or science? Which
of the two is it that is shaping the thought of the world?"[56] He would go
on to further question the value of scholarship for the sake of scholarship.

> To use language which this mercantile community can under-
> stand, . . . we have been trying to sell goods for which there is no
> market. . . . In this practical community of men, hastening to be rich,

we found no sympathy. . . . But few American youth . . . care to saunter to the fountains of knowledge through the pleasant winding of their flowery path. The practical branches must take the lead and bear the weight, and the ornamental must follow.[57]

Adopting the same philosophy as Draper was Francis Wayland at Brown University, who suggested that "the colleges were becoming more and more superficial. . . . As efforts were made to accommodate new subjects within the old framework, all subjects were offered in diluted quantities, and one consequence was that the colleges were turning out men who were not expert in anything."[58]

He proposed, instead, "a radical change . . . [in] the system of collegiate instruction," proposing reforms, among others, such as an end to the fixed four-year course study and allowing students to allot time to their studies according to its utility.[59] Wayland's proposals would be made with the objective of bringing the American college into focus with the main social and economic developments of the new era.

Ultimately, traditional institutions of higher education would adopt the Tappan model over the sentiments of Draper and Wayland. Yale, for example, developed a School of Applied Chemistry as a section of the newly authorized Department of Philosophy and the Arts.[60] Rather than separate and emphasize areas of study over others, colleges worked to infuse learning from a vast spectrum of studies into a grand liberal arts education model that is in many ways still in existence today.

For those who did attempt to apply Wayland's proposals, the reforms would crumble quickly, returning the institutions to the safe ways of the past. For example, in light of calls to adopt Wayland's model, James H. Thornwell, president of South Carolina College, asserted that "while others are veering to the popular pressure . . . let it be our aim to make Scholars and not sappers, or miners—apothecaries—doctors or farmers."[61]

This debate over land-grant colleges was but a small chapter in a century-old debate over the objectives and ideal model of higher education, one that continues on even today. The search for a rationale of the land-grant colleges only worked to intensify controversy between popularists, who would provide only practical technical education and classicists, who would offer a multidisciplinary education that predominates today as a liberal arts education.

Eventually, the classicists prevailed, establishing that "the idea of an American University is a central school of Philosophy, . . . surrounded by the Professional Schools, embracing not only the Departments of Law, Medicine, and Divinity, but the Normal School for the education of teachers, and Schools of Agriculture and the Useful Arts."[62] The American University was conceived, and largely survives today as

> not a high school . . . nor an academy of sciences, nor an industrial school which we are charged to build. . . . The university is the most comprehensive term that can be employed to indicate a foundation for the promotion and diffusion of knowledge—a group of agencies organized to advance the arts and sciences of every sort, and train young men as scholars for all the intellectual callings of life.[63]

In other words, the American University, as it was conceived then and as it exists today, hinges overwhelmingly upon a liberal arts education that emphasizes the art of thinking at the expense of practical job market training.

The nineteenth century successfully conceived an infant liberal arts degree and built the crib of an American University where it would slowly grow into adolescence. However, it would be the twentieth century that supplied the critical elements to turn this maturing but controlled system into the untamable beast that threatens to destroy us today.

"The decade around the turn of the twentieth century witnessed the flourishing of the American research university and the emergence of public sector institutions as leaders in educational quality."[64] In the following two or three decades, "institutions of higher education vastly increased in scale, particularly those in the public sector, and public sector institutions greatly expanded their enrollments relative to their private counterparts."[65]

During this time, "an increasing number of subjects taught in colleges and universities became subdivided and specialized, and those who taught began to define themselves as occupying separate, specialized fields."[66] The old model of lumping fields within fields would soon be a relic. The historic Yale School of Applied Chemistry that was born within the Department of Philosophy and the Arts was no more.

While the number of subjects and their scope expanded, higher education developed into "an organization composed of individuals devoted to a particular learned discipline or branch or group of disciplines in the humanities, social sciences, or natural sciences and primarily committed to the study and acquisition of knowledge in such discipline."[67]

These efforts were supported by new legislative measures such as the Smith-Hughes Act in 1917, which firmly established the funding necessary for publicly supported vocational schools. This not only worked to successfully confine the previously expanding for-profit market, sending the for-profit colleges into decline, but also more importantly, it solidified the movement toward separate and expanded fields of study, as well as the future of the state college, where this model would be embraced more quickly than anywhere else.[68]

Although subjects were gradually split into their own departments, resources, and specialized professors, the general liberal arts degree still prevailed by requiring courses of study across departments in a multidisciplinary education. For example, students majoring in the social sciences would be required to take classes in the humanities and natural sciences.

English, math, history, and science, although more clearly defined by separate departments, would still be required for graduation. In other words, the structure of modern higher education had been transformed, but the liberal arts mentality still prevailed. Put another way, specialization won the battle, but ultimately lost the war.

While initiatives like the land-grant movement and the Smith-Hughes Act helped to shape the modern mold for the course of study and increased access to the working class with modest initiatives, higher education in 1940 paled in comparison to the market that exists today. In 1940, enrollment had grown to over 1.4 million students nationwide, constituting 9.1 percent of the population of people ages 18–24.[69] However, these numbers are dwarfed by college enrollment today, which in 2012 reached 20.6 million students nationwide, constituting 41 percent of the population ages 18–24.[70]

Consequently, we must ask ourselves why—why did higher education in America change so fundamentally over the course of the following decades? How could so much change occur in so little time, relative to the modest progress achieved over the three hundred years previous? Ultimately, the answer lies with the United States shifting from a modern nation to a world power in the aftermath of World War II and its posturing against the Soviet Union in the early chapters of the Cold War.

With the Soviet Union emerging as a preeminent economic and military power in the post-war twentieth century, the United States began to subsidize the cost of attending college to give the masses the opportunity to think and innovate with a college education. With the GI Bill (1944), the National Defense Education Act (1958), and the Higher Education Act (1965), Congress laid the foundation for educating large amounts of the population with the intended purpose of strengthening the economy, improving innovation, and ensuring national security throughout the Cold War.

This surge of financial support for institutions of higher education "expanded access to college to growing numbers of Americans from across the income spectrum," enabling people from modest backgrounds "to enjoy occupational choices and a standard of living their parents could only have dreamed of."[71]

As we will go into in further detail in later chapters, federal higher education initiatives in the mid-twentieth century and beyond have launched higher education to levels unforeseeable just a century ago. Armed with the term *college- and career-ready*, many are calling for universal higher education in the United States.[72]

Think about it in these terms: "In 1704, Worcester County, New York, there were but six families that could spare their children enough time to learn more than reading and writing."[73] Three hundred years ago, only a handful of privileged families could afford to send their sons off to the equivalent of finishing schools. Today, more than 20 million students attend college, and people are still clamoring for more—more access, more fields of study, more shiny buildings, more five-star dining options, more lavish residence halls—more.

This chapter tells the story of how higher education in the United States began and slowly developed into the modern era. The remainder of this book will strive to tackle the problem that faces us today—the same one created by the roots that have been described in this opening chapter. Our problem is a web of misguided priorities of institutions, excessive greed of lenders, the shortsightedness of Congress, and the ignorance of students, which has trapped tens of millions of people under $1.3 trillion of college debt. It is the purpose of the remaining

chapters to root out the causes of these problems and to offer solutions
before it is too late.

ESSENTIAL TAKEAWAYS

Higher education began in America with limited access and a parochial
purpose. Over time, access gradually expanded and the purpose shifted
from parochial to civil by the late eighteenth century, to practical and
industrial by the early nineteenth century, and eventually to a liberal
arts model by the latter half of the nineteenth century that still predominates today. Although many clamored for a practical higher education
model built upon the premise of serving the needs of society, colleges
ultimately embraced a model of scholarship that would promote personal fulfillment of individuals.

While access remained overwhelmingly limited through the first half
of the twentieth century, modern legislative initiatives during the early
years of the Cold War opened access to millions of students in the
subsequent decades as a way to ensure national security and promote
public utility. Accepting these subsidies under few conditions, however,
colleges never embraced these legislative objectives and continued on
their mission of scholarship and personal fulfillment at the expense of
practical skills training and public interest. It is this blank check of
subsidies with a lack of practical focus that ultimately sowed the seeds
for the modern financial crisis of higher education today.

2

TANKED BY RANK

We now know how colleges *were*. The remaining focus of this book will be to examine how colleges *are*, as they exist today, and *ought to be* moving forward. Nonprofit higher education is split into two subcategories—private and public institutions—which are then classified as certificate, associate's, bachelor's, master's, and doctoral programs. Together, they account for 88 percent of enrollment in the United States, with the remaining 12 percent attending for-profit colleges.[1]

The public college sector makes up approximately 80 percent of total college enrollment, 45 percent, or approximately 9.3 million, of whom are enrolled in community colleges that house two-year associate's degree programs.[2] The other 35 percent of students in public higher education attend four-year colleges, or 7.2 million students. Meanwhile, its private nonprofit counterparts account for only 8 percent of total national enrollment, or 1.7 million students.[3]

Although titles such as "nonprofit" might bring with it connotations of "inexpensive" and "affordable," these presuppositions are incorrect. Since 1966, tuition, room, and board have increased from less than $2,500 to over $38,500 at private colleges in 2016; from less than $1,500 to over $24,000 at public colleges for out-of-state students in 2016; and from less than $500 to more than $9,500 at public colleges for in-state students in 2016.[4]

When all is said and done, cost of attendance (COA) between 1966 and 2016 has surged approximately 1,580 percent at four-year private colleges, 2,050 percent at four-year out-of-state public colleges, and 2,720 percent at four-year in-state colleges in 2016.[5]

Although it is true that many of the recent cost increases in public higher education are attributed to cuts in state and federal funding, and while most students do not pay full sticker price, the amount that students are paying has increased nonetheless.

To the former, students quite frankly do not care *why* they are paying more; they only care that they *are* paying more. Furthermore, although reductions in government aid have magnified the problem, public colleges also engage in many of the same wasteful practices that private colleges do, which remains a crucial element of the rising trend in public higher education costs.

As for the latter, students may not be paying sticker price; however, as the sticker price continues to go up, the relative "reduced" price continues to slide upward as a result. Between government and private aid, most students do not pay the full advertised cost.

For example, if the COA of a private college in the 1990s was roughly $25,000, a student was only paying a fraction of that. However, subsi-

	Private 4-Year	Public 4-Year (out-of-state)	Public 4-Year (in-state)
1966	2,456	1,171	360
1976	4,715	2,067	689
1986	12,278	4,469	1,651
1996	23,520	7,792	3,323
2006	28,896	15,253	6,836
2016	38,762	24,015	9,803

Figure 2.1.   Cost of Attendance Since 1966 (in Current Dollars).   Source: National Center for Education Statistics, "Table 320: Average Undergraduate Tuition and Fees and Room and Board Rates Charged for Full-Time Students in Degree-Granting Institutions, by Type and Control of Institution: 1964–65 through 2006–07," U.S. Department of Education Institute of Education Sciences, 2008, https://nces.ed.gov/ programs/digest/d07/tables/dt07_320.asp (accessed February 20, 2016); Travis Mitchell, "See 20 Years of Tuition Growth at National Universities," U.S. News & World Report, July 29, 2015, www.usnews.com/education/best-colleges/paying-for-college/ articles/2015/07/29/chart-see-20-years-of-tuition-growth-at-national-universities (accessed February 20, 2016).

dies have not kept pace with annual price increases. With the same college education now costing roughly $40,000 today, the same or even greater financial aid from 1996 will create a much greater deficit to the student in 2016. In other words, $15,000 in aid went a lot further in 1996 than it does in 2016.

Consequently, the national student loan debt has surged to an unprecedented $1.3 trillion,[6] translating to an average college debt burden of over $35,000 per student.[7] To put this figure into perspective, gross domestic product (GDP) in Spain, Mexico, South Korea, and Australia are all roughly $1.3 trillion.[8] Thus, our national college debt bubble is essentially the same size as entire economies of other major industrialized countries throughout the world.

As the cost of college continues to rise at exponential levels, academics have probed for answers explaining why this trend exists. Research surrounding these questions suggests that there is no single factor that exclusively accounts for these price increases, as public and private institutions are fundamentally different in ways ranging from their subsidization to their student enrollment.

Despite these differences, the snowballing price trend within both sectors can be traced back to a mutual incentive that drives many of the cost increases that exist today. Therefore, it will be the purpose of the following two chapters to highlight the two-fold phenomenon that explains *why* private and public institutions are increasing costs. Additionally, I will offer possible explanations that account for *how* colleges encourage the phenomenon that drives up the price of both private and public higher education.

A closer look at nonprofit institutions reveals that while the objective to promote a higher quality of education exists, there is a more deeply rooted and self-interested enterprise at work. This most fundamental priority of nonprofit colleges is increasingly referred to as "prestige maximization," which stands as the first part of a two-fold phenomenon accounting for why private and public institutions are increasing costs.[9]

Prestige maximization is ultimately born from a highly competitive college market, where applicants strive to attend the most prominent universities as a means to be competitive in an increasingly demanding job market. One of the primary ways that students distinguish desirable universities from those that are not is through a series of rankings, published annually by credible organizations such as *U.S. News &*

World Report (*USN&WR*). Consequently, "when published rankings influence potential students' perceptions of the quality of institutions, the institutions have a strong incentive to try to influence the rankings."[10]

An investigation conducted by the Davis Educational Foundation, which collected a series of responses from seventy college and university presidents, fully supports this notion. One university president explained that "governing boards and administrators seek to influence the rankings," which "have been one of the most powerful (and pernicious) forces driving colleges."[11] Therefore, administrators strive to maximize the value of their institutions by the criteria of how colleges are ranked, with the hope that their ranking will go up and attract a better applicant pool as a result.

An analysis of how *USN&WR* ranks the value of a college is crucial to understanding the phenomenon of prestige maximization. Since 1999, *USN&WR's* college ranking criteria and weights emphasize what universities offer to students while they are enrolled (inputs), while weighing very little on student outcomes that can be used as a measurement for judging how effective these inputs are at preparing students for a career (outputs).

In terms of these inputs, each specific weight falls into one of two general categories. Under general *Financial Commitments*, "Faculty Resources" account for 20 percent, "Financial Resources" 10 percent, and "Alumni Giving" 5 percent.[12] In the other broad classification of *Student Satisfaction and Perceived Quality*, "Academic Reputation" is weighted 22.5 percent, "Graduation and Retention Rates" 22.5 percent, and "Student Selectivity" 12.5 percent.[13]

Based upon this criteria, colleges who wish to sustain their position or rise in the rankings are incentivized to spend more money on many of the inputs under the *Financial Commitments* category. While some criteria are straightforward, other weights are split into a number of factors that better explain how college prices are affected. To understand this, it is worth mentioning the sub-factors for these multidimensional criteria.

The "Faculty Resources" section, for example, is comprised of "faculty compensation," "percent of faculty with terminal degree in their field," "percent of faculty that is employed full time," "student-faculty ratio," and "class size."[14] Meanwhile, other factors, such as "Alumni

Giving," are based upon a single factor. But even though these factors seem simple, they are not. Continuing with "Alumni Giving," this weight is "calculated by dividing the number of alumni donors during a given academic year by the number of alumni on record for that same year."[15]

Additionally, much of this increased spending ultimately works to inflate the subcategories under *Student Satisfaction and Perceived Quality* by offering services that both enhance institutional reputation with frill factors and increase the number of prospective applications as a result. The collective theme here is that rankings promote a constant state of expansion as the norm for how colleges compete.

In the midst of this grand rankings scheme, the only output weight is graduation rate performance, which makes up only 7.5 percent of the total criteria.[16] In other words, the performance of students once they leave—meaning if the student is employed, earning a decent salary, able to pay off their student debt, functioning as a contributing member of society—only influences 7.5 percent of a college's rank.

Here rests one of the core problems with higher education today. Prospective college students, a majority being young men and women only seventeen or eighteen years old, have been sold the idea that going to college is the ticket to success. With a skewed faith in the system, these same students fail to realize that colleges are judged overwhelmingly not by the long-term success of their students, but by what is offered during their time in college. Put another way, students' faith in the system is based upon a lie, and rankings are one of the cornerstones used to prop up this misrepresentation.

Because colleges rely heavily on their rank to sway prospective students to apply, colleges are put in a very difficult position. "On the one hand, the institutions would like to reduce their costs to keep tuition increases down. On the other hand, if any institution unilaterally did so, it would adversely affect its ranking because the ranking is based on how much it spends."[17]

Even colleges that do not wish to pursue spending as a means to compete for high rankings are eventually forced to as a result of an invasive trickle-down phenomenon. As one college president explains:

> One of the difficulties of the perception that "Price Equals Quality"
> is that highly-selective well-endowed schools can raise tuition with-

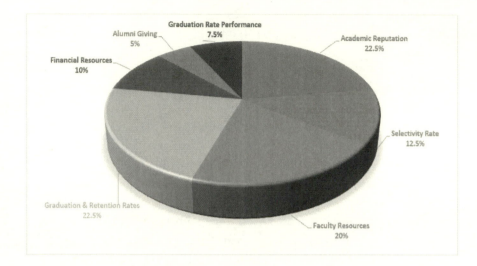

Figure 2.2.   USN&WR Ranking Criteria.   *Source: Robert Morse and Eric Brooks, "Best Colleges Ranking Criteria and Weights," U.S.* News and World Report, *September 8, 2015, www.usnews.com/education/best-colleges/articles/ranking-criteria-and-weights (accessed December 19, 2015).*

out losing talented students. The demand for entrance to these schools is so high they could, if they wanted, fill their classes many times over with full tuition paying students. The "elite" schools in effect establish the boundary for tuition rates for all schools. The less wealthy schools can increase their tuition at a faster rate than they might otherwise because a higher price boundary has been set. . . . It is a vicious cycle.[18]

Due to the fact that ranking criteria places such a great deal of emphasis on institutional inputs, when added to the trickle-down effect that occurs in relation to forced spending for survival, colleges have no choice but to resort to "increasing amenities of both academic and recreational life, as competition driven by a desire for prestige" prevails as the predominant business model.[19]

While this may seem conclusive enough, in that colleges are incentivized to spend more, there is an additional component at work that explains this trend. Not only are colleges encouraged to increase spending, but also as a recent report filed through the Research Institute for Higher Education indicates, colleges are meticulous in allocating funds so to statistically maximize prestige amidst the competition between colleges to rise in the ranks.

Identifying institutional allocations along a "possible prestige curve," the authors conclude that colleges "demonstrate a mechanism through which optimal allocation arrangement of resources is sought by an institution of higher education in pursuit of the highest institutional prestige."[20] This further demonstrates that prestige maximization is considered by colleges to be a primary objective when considering institutional budgets.

In addition to the competition between institutions to attract students, it is worth noting that similar competition exists internally within the college itself, further compounding the college spending conundrum created by ranking incentives. Described as "organized anarchies," competition exists at numerous tiers of any given college, beginning with each field that is offered. Within fields, there is competition between departments, and within departments arises competition between faculty members, "all pursuing different objectives."[21]

At every level, interests compete for a share of the institutional budget under the "financial resources" section of *USN&WR*'s ranking criteria, which is largely responsible for funding academic projects that are conducted by any given field, department, or faculty member.[22] While smaller factions within the collective institution wrangle over funds to build upon their individual programs, administrators continue to face the objective of improving upon the college rank as a whole.

Therefore, colleges have the dual-incentive of continuing to grow their "financial resource"[23] expenditures, as it not only satisfies faculty demands for more research, instructional, and student services funding, but is also considered to be a greater commitment to students by *USN&WR* standards under "financial resources," raising the institution's rank as a result.

Born from this is a nonprofit higher education industry that operates not much differently from its for-profit counterpart. Whether it is the prestige-orientation of the former or the profit-seeking of the latter, these two distinct sectors suffer from the same natural urge to grow with little or no restraint. From this, it becomes clear that the prestige of nonprofit colleges is costly to students in a way that is similar to the profit generation of for-profit colleges.

As the standard of unprecedented college growth over the last several decades has been established as the new competitive norm, construction projects have inevitably set the pace for expansion. College buildings "contribute directly to the educational mission of the institution through the classrooms and research laboratories that it houses," as well as providing "infrastructure for the institution's support and administrative services."[24] It is from this understanding that "institutions have operated on the assumption that the more they build, expand, and diversify, the more they will persist and prosper."[25]

The significant expansion of academic, science, residence, and library buildings in particular can be explained for several reasons. Going back to the "financial resources" category of *USN&WR* ratings, it makes sense that the capacity for "financial resources" is largely dependent upon the physical amount of space that a college has at its disposal to house the classrooms, laboratories, student services, and administrative services that make up the financial resources of a university.

Consequently, raising the rank of a college cannot be achieved through the "financial resources" category if there are not enough buildings to facilitate such an expansion. Jean-Baptiste Say explains this phenomenon with Say's Law, asserting that "supply creates its own demand."[26]

Working from an "if you build it, they will come" philosophy, colleges quickly fill new space with additional services and programs to attract more students to apply. This ties back to the college rankings in two additional ways, on top of simply increasing the amount of "financial resources."

The first can be drawn back to the fact that a majority of these projects are funded partly through contributions from alum to the university. By increasing the number of building projects, and diversifying the purposes of these buildings, the university has a greater likelihood of capturing more gifts from enthused alum, expanding upon the 5 percent of "alumni giving" in the college ranking criteria.

Second, the 12.5 percent of "student selectivity" in the ranking criteria can also be influenced as a result of additional building. By expanding and diversifying, colleges have the capacity to attract not only more alum donors, but also the attention of more potential applicants as well. As colleges continue to persuade more prospective students to apply, while admitting only a small proportion of this new pool of applicants, the college's "student selectivity" ratio has the potential to decrease significantly. Consequently, lower "student selectivity" translates into a higher rating under *USN&WR* standards, further helping the college to rise in the ranks.

The emphasis on capital building projects might also be explained by the internal competition of "organized anarchies." Space is indicative not only of an individual faculty member's prestige at a university, but of entire departments as well. So much so that there have been cases when departments will not allow faculty members within their department to relinquish space, even if he or she wants to.[27] Given the immense pressure from both of these factors, more so in the former than the latter, colleges across the country have worked to sustain and expand upon the rate of capital building projects.

For reasons we will explore in the subsequent chapters, spending on construction projects, which include but are not limited to academic, science, library, and residence hall buildings, began its rapid escalation in the mid-1990s. From an expenditure of $6.1 billion on college construction projects in 1995, national college spending on construction surpassed $7 billion by 2000, jumping to $9.8 billion in 2001.[28] This trend continued until its peak in 2006, when colleges reported spending approximately $15 billion on building projects, almost three times more than recorded only a decade earlier.[29]

From this exponential financial investment in college infrastructure, "U.S. higher educational facilities of all types expanded from 74 million square feet in starts in 1981 . . . to 223 million square feet [in 2008], or almost three times the level of 1981."[30]

Despite the incredible surge in college infrastructure, this era of rapid expansion has slowed significantly since the implosion of the housing bubble in 2008. Following this event, colleges saw immediate declines in contributions from alum, who were now less free to contribute money to colleges due to broad economic uncertainty. As a result, national college construction expenditures fell to $10.7 billion by 2009, and "it has stayed at that level since, rebounding to just over $11 billion in 2010."[31]

Although it seemed as though college construction spending was stabilizing amidst a suffering economy, it was not until recent government budget cuts that colleges recorded their lowest building expenditures since 2001.

Due to the significant state subsidization of public colleges, public institutions of higher education bore the brunt of these cuts. Reductions "in FY 2010 were much larger than in other years during the decade, averaging single-year declines of 9 percent to 13 percent at public four-year institutions and 15 percent at public community colleges."[32] These declines, "which averaged between $600 and $1,000 per student, resulted in the lowest per-student state and local funding in the decade,"[33] further promoting the decline in college infrastructure until hitting a low point of $9.7 billion in 2012.[34]

In addition to the cumulative 17.4 percent reduction in state aid to colleges over the course of the recession, amounting to $15.2 billion, "there has also been a 12 percent increase in public college enrollment during this same period. That means the average public college gets a tax subsidy of only $6,600 per student, down from $9,300 just five years ago," as a result of having less total revenue to pay for more students.[35]

While these reductions have fallen hardest upon state schools, private colleges have also seen fewer grants for capital building projects. When compounded with declines in contributions and endowments, private schools have been forced to take on long-term debt in addition to borrowing "bridge funds to finance a project until the anticipated gifts have all been received," as well as extending short lines of credit to "help cover operating expenses."[36] Nonetheless, even with credit lines and long-term debt being extended, public colleges in particular have been reluctant to keep up with the rapid pace of expansion seen in years prior to 2008.

This period of depressed building, however, is expected to be short-lived. With the Dow and S&P 500 hitting record highs,[37] unemployment falling to a five-year low of 7 percent,[38] and GDP annualized rates rebounding to encouraging levels,[39] the economy is showing sure signs of recovery, restoring grants and contributions to their pre-recession levels. Recent figures indicate that this prediction is correct, as college construction expenditures saw their first increase since 2006, recovering to $10.1 billion in FY 2013. In other words, colleges have quickly returned to their old habits of excessive capital building projects to continue upon their model of growth.

ESSENTIAL TAKEAWAYS

After identifying the incredible surge in college costs in recent decades, we begin to look for reasons that might explain why. As part of a two-fold phenomenon, prestige maximization stands as the driving force behind college activity, as it is the primary way colleges compete in the marketplace. Due to the misguided emphasis that has been placed on institutional inputs and not on the output of post-graduation student performance, colleges are incentivized to compete by spending more and offering more each year.

Compounded by the cannibalizing nature of departments and faculty competing for the largest possible share of funds and space, colleges continue to raise prices and build more as a way to generate new service offerings to students and faculty alike. Consequently, the colleges have adopted a motto of *MORE* that is unsustainable over the long term.

3

PENNILESS FOR PERKS

Although the sheer amount of money allocated toward construction projects is indicative of the rising costs of higher education, further examination reveals an additional component to college building projects in recent years. The second prong of the two-fold phenomenon constitutes an "amenities war" between colleges. In other words, colleges compete not only on the volume of what is offered, but also by the curb appeal or frill factors of their campuses as well.

This is well illustrated by continuing with the examination of building projects at colleges and universities. Despite the impact of recession forces decreasing the total amount of money spent on building projects since 2007, the cost per square foot of these projects has continued to increase steadily at an exponential rate.

Data collected from academic buildings under construction in 2012 reveals that the median cost of these projects was $31 million, or an average of $388 per square foot.[1] This figure, when compared to the approximate cost of $125 per square foot in 1997 and $206 per square foot in 2007 of similar buildings, indicates a 310 percent increase since 1997 and a 149 percent increase from 2007.[2]

Additionally, the 2012 median cost per square foot among science buildings was approximately $509, "making these the most expensive buildings to construct based on cost and size."[3] This is seen as a 305 percent spike from the 1997 average of $167 per square foot, and a 176 percent increase from the 2007 average of $290 per square foot.[4]

Library buildings have also seen significant increases over this same time period, rising from $138 per square foot in 1997 and $253 per square foot in 2007, to $322 per square foot in 2012.[5] This signifies a growth of 233 percent since 1997 and an increase of 127 percent from 2007.

A final set of buildings that are indicative of higher infrastructure costs per square foot are residence hall buildings, which rose from $75 per square foot in 1997 and $150 per square foot in 2007, to $245 per square foot in 2012.[6] This represents a 326 percent increase from 1997 as well as a 163 percent surge since 2007.

When averaged together, the cost of college infrastructure projects has increased by 294 percent since 1997 and 154 percent since 2007, representing an average annual increase of 25 percent in the cost of college building projects since 1997.

Considering these statistics, why have college administrators continued to increase spending per square foot on building projects, even after the post-financial-crisis cuts in private and public funding for college infrastructure? Statements pulled from the Davis Educational Foundation offer insight into the broader qualitative concepts that work to support the data collected in quantitative studies on college construction projects. "Irrespective of the size and types of institutions . . . there is more pressure to add and improve than to scale back," creating a "mantra for growth and improvement that is *constant*."[7]

As one university president suggests:

> In higher education the incentives to compete on quality are high and the incentives to compete on price are low. . . . People assume that when a college saves on cost its price comes down or at least doesn't go up as much. But this never happens because there is every incentive to plow that savings into increased quality.[8]

This competition, as another university administrator suggests, is born from the fact that "consumers—students and parents—expect more, have less to spend, have greater options, and can choose from an over-capacity of 'teaching' institutions and opportunities of various kinds," adding that while "higher education offers the experience that parents and students have come to expect beyond their education, there is a cost for this experience."[9]

As a consequence of growing demands from prospective students, colleges are encouraged to offer more amenities, or non-instructional services, in order to remain competitive. Taken from a statistical study that quantifies the general qualitative statements made by college administrators in the Davis Educational Foundation brief, a report filed to the National Bureau of Economic Research by three University of Michigan professors explains this development in detail.

The report begins with the basic premise that colleges are faced with the task of determining "different levels of academic versus amenity spending" in order to maximize the number of applicants to their institutions.[10] Working from the assumption that "individuals compare potential utility received from attending each college and choose to attend the college that maximizes their utility,"[11] the authors conduct surveys to estimate student demand, using the standard deviation of a four-point scale to determine how important "academics (courses and reputation), costs (low cost, financial aid), and social amenities (athletics, social life)" are to each student.[12]

Analyzing data collected in an IPEDS College Finance report filed by the Delta Cost Project, the authors relate the data from their own student demand surveys to understand whether there is a correlation

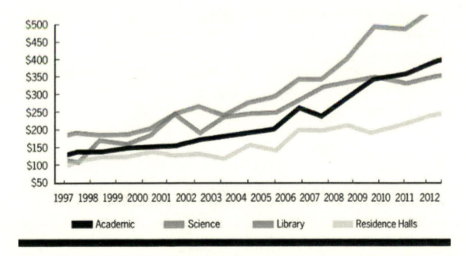

Figure 3.1. Trends in the Cost of College Construction Projects per sq. ft.
Source: Paul Abramson, "2013 College Construction Report: Proceeding with Caution," 6.

between the two. After reviewing how four-year public and nonprofit private schools have adjusted "institutional spending on consumption amenities," with "expenditures on instruction and academic support per FTE as a measure of the institution's academic quality," the authors come to the conclusion that there is a definite correlation. [13]

Academic quality measures included "expenses for all forms of instruction (i.e., academic, occupational, vocational, adult basic education and extension sessions, credit and non-credit) as well as spending on libraries, museums, galleries, etc.," while accounting for consumption amenities as "current spending on student services and auxiliary enterprises." [14]

These two categories are further explained by classifying spending on student services as "spending on admissions, registrar, student records, student activities, cultural events, student newspapers, intramural athletics, and student organizations," while auxiliary expenditures are considered to be "operating expenditures for residence halls, food services, student health services, intercollegiate athletics, college unions, and college stores." [15]

Following a clearly defined and deliberately executed study of these relationships, the authors note a series of conclusive findings. They begin by determining that "on average, students marginally value institutions' spending on consumption attributes and the academic ability of their peers, but do not value spending on instruction." [16] The report goes on to say that the willingness to pay (WTP) for consumption amenities is "positive for most members of the sample . . . yet the same is only true for instruction for a limited number of individuals," who were restricted to the category of "very high-achieving" by the model's standard. [17]

Thus, colleges face an implicit trade-off in terms of budgetary allocation. Increases in instructional spending will attract high-achieving students, but may deter enrollment from a broader student body, while more amenities spending attracts all types of students. [18] Claiming that the report has "documented a substantial enrollment response to spending on student services and auxiliary enterprises" by measuring the ratio of consumption amenities spending to instructional spending between 1992 to 2007, the authors conclude that "preference-induced demand pressure explains 16 percent of the variation in spending priorities across four-year institutions." [19]

So far, it has been established that college rankings encourage institutions to increase spending to the point that the choice of raising spending levels is no longer left to the discretion of the individual institution. Rather, a system driven by an infatuation with rankings poses a serious threat to any institution that unilaterally refuses to conform to spending pressures that are driven by rank. This rank-induced spending is compounded with the demand-pressure of prospective students who are progressively more demanding of amenities when choosing a college to enroll in.

While colleges might label their response to these demands with generic terms like "student and administrative services," or "college expansion and diversification," as to make these allocations sound vital to the college learning experience, reality suggests that large-scale building projects and excessive luxury services are meant to seduce prospective students into applying.

This dual phenomenon has led to what some are calling the "country-clubization" of the American university, particularly through social amenities such as "dormitories, dining facilities, student unions, medical facilities, and athletic facilities."[20] Richard Vedder, a distinguished professor of economics at Ohio University, suggests that "in the zeal to get students," colleges are "going after them on the basis of recreational amenities like great athletic centers and spectacular student union buildings."[21] While this might seem like an unwarranted charge by Professor Vedder, the buildings and services that he critiques are sprouting up on campuses all around the country.

Part of an "unremitting arms race," George Washington University has recently finished construction on a "new $130 million 'super dorm' and a $33 million textile museum."[22] Likewise, "the University of Pennsylvania's gym recently underwent a $10 million renovation project to include an Olympic-sized swimming pool, co-ed sauna, juice bar, golf simulator, and rock-climbing wall," while Kenyon College has recently opened a "$70 million athletic center with similar country club features."[23]

Elite institutions, however, are not the only colleges that have engaged in the perpetual arms race on amenities. During the summer of 2012 alone, Penn State University sanctioned fifteen campus improvement projects, ranging from the renovation of the South Residence Halls, to capital building projects like the Eva J. Pell Laboratory for

Advanced Biological Research.[24] Not only the scope but also the luxurious nature of these projects offers a possible explanation for why the cost per square foot of college construction projects has increased by an annual rate of 25 percent,[25] perpetuating the trend of an ever-growing cost to higher education for an "increasingly demanding clientele."[26]

One must not forget that although alum contributions and state grants might cover a majority of the initial construction costs, there is rarely revenue to finance the long-term operation and maintenance of these facilities, which can then easily be transferred to students through tuition and fee increases.

With the erection of elaborate college construction projects on campuses around the country, many of them arguably unnecessary to fulfill the task of enhancing the quality of education, these buildings have been filled with an equally unnecessary number of administrative and student services personnel at colleges as well. As Suzanne Mettler highlights, colleges are increasing the number of student support services, "such as mental health counseling and writing tutors."[27]

Statistics reveal that this investment over the last twenty years has had a significant impact both on how colleges operate as well as on tuition over time. "Between 1993 and 2007, the number of full-time administrators per 100 students at America's leading universities grew by 39 percent, while the number of employees engaged in teaching, research, or service (IRS) only grew by 17.6 percent."[28] This amounts to a 61 percent increase in inflation-adjusted spending for administrators over this same period.

These figures can be further broken down by institution type. At private four-year universities, the proportion of administrators to IRS personnel remained relatively the same, both increasing by approximately 40 percent between 1993 and 2007. However, this has only worked to solidify the disproportion of administration to IRS, the former rising to 15.8 per 100 students while the latter only climbed to 11.5 per 100 students.[29] This proportionate discrepancy is even more severe at public universities, which experienced a 39 percent increase in administration since 1993, while only allowing for a 9.8 percent increase in IRS personnel over this same period.[30]

Speaking to this point, a Bain & Company report on financially sustainable universities substantiates these statistics. It claims that not only are institutions' long-term debt "increasing at an average rate of approximately 12 percent, and their average annual interest expense growing at almost twice the rate of their instruction-related expense," but "administrative and student services costs are growing faster than instructional costs."[31] Further analysis suggests that the increase in instructors is primarily derived from adjuncts, as accounting for 82.7 percent of the increase at private schools and 31.5 percent at public colleges.[32]

The University of California–Davis stands as a prime example of this trend. Employing 2,358 full-time administrators at its central office in Oakland, UC–Davis has created ten divisions in the Office of the President, fifty-five "managerial-type employees" in external relations, and hundreds more in the business operations and academic affairs divisions.[33] This has ultimately led to a 318.8 percent increase in administration between 1993 and 2007, while IRS staff actually *decreased* by 4.5 percent over the same time period.[34]

In addition to national upward trends in the sheer number of administrators and IRS personnel that are employed, the cost of these services are also on the rise. Not surprisingly, "the cost of administration for each student, like the number of administrators per student, has been increasing dramatically."[35] While Wake Forest, for example, has increased administrative spending per student by more than 600 percent between 1993 and 2007, Harvard has also demonstrated similar spending increases of 300 percent over the same period of time.[36]

Even public colleges have committed an exorbitant amount of resources toward administration, as ASU increased per student administrative spending by 46.3 percent, NAU by 36.5 percent, and UA by 28.8 percent.[37] These figures signify that universities of all types are suffering from what some academics are calling an "administrative bloat."

While institutions continue to allocate more resources toward administration, simultaneously depriving students of adequate resources on IRS, college students continue to pay more for elements that might "contribute to a student's wellbeing while they are enrolled, but do not directly increase productivity, or earnings, later in life."[38]

Consistent with the frill theme of unnecessary recreational amenities and administrative bloat is the existence of many amusing yet ludicrous courses and majors. For example, if you find yourself at the University of Connecticut, you have the opportunity of majoring in "Puppetry."[39] Other comparable majors include "Popular Culture" at Bowling Green

State University,[40] "Adventure Education" at Plymouth State University,[41] and "Family Enterprise" at Stetson University.[42]

Although these majors seem strange and tangibly inapplicable to general society, individual courses within other majors are even further removed from reality. Whether it's the "Philosophy of *Star Trek*" at Georgetown University,[43] "Fat Studies" at the University of Maryland,[44] or "Science of Superheroes" at the University of California at Irvine,[45] courses such as these do little to "directly increase productivity, or earnings, later in life."[46]

Whether it is buildings, administrative bloat, or bizarre course studies, colleges have illustrated a consistent theme: a reliable method of competing is to overwhelm students with as many frill factors as possible, even though these products and services will do little to nothing to offer long-term tangible value to the student once they have graduated.

ESSENTIAL TAKEAWAYS

The scope of these recent trends leads some to believe that colleges operate in a market where the only hope of survival hinges upon a willingness to continually expand, despite the cost burden to students. Once forced by ranking criteria to engage in high rates of spending, colleges are then driven by an amenity demand from prospective applicants to draw money away from instruction and full-time faculty. This is done with the purpose of providing more luxurious building and renovation projects, only to fill them with a disproportionate number of unnecessary administrative and student services personnel.

"Colleges and universities are held back in their efforts to implement cost efficiency savings by a tendency for prospective students and rating systems to focus on activities and inputs, rather than upon effectiveness in delivering educational outcomes."[47] Consequently, as one university president suggests, "the model for most universities and colleges is no longer feasible," creating a financial bubble that threatens to explode with unknown rippling effects if this growing trend is not reversed.

4

LENDING ROOTS

Inception of Greed

So far, we have examined the establishment and evolution of higher education in America, in addition to identifying several market forces that have incentivized colleges to increase spending over the last several decades. The question of how students are *able to pay* for these spending increases has yet to be determined.

Before venturing into possible remedies to correct the "changing priorities of colleges,"[1] we must analyze this question by examining sources of revenue other than government subsidies. This inevitably leads the next three chapters of our discussion to the heart of the private student lending industry. We will first examine the evolution of the student lending industry from its origin, and examine how its transformation, led by Sallie Mae, has systematically facilitated the progressive increase in the cost of college, particularly over the last two decades.

Following WWII, three milestone pieces of Congressional legislation, spanning a twenty-year period, were implemented to increase college enrollment through a series of financial assistance programs. Produced from separate motives, ranging from national security measures to promoting equal opportunity, several bills were passed to expand access to higher education.

The first was passed in 1944 as the Servicemen's Readjustment Act, also commonly known as the GI Bill. Different from the latter two measures, the GI Bill was enacted to reward veterans who had served

and sacrificed for their country. Intended to help servicemen and -
women assimilate back into American domestic life, the GI Bill extended higher education opportunities to thousands of people who
would have otherwise struggled to "readjust" upon their return.

Because paying for college was the primary factor barring the majority of returning veterans from applying to college, the federal government issued up to $500 to each veteran per school year as a way to help
cover costs ranging from tuition to books.[2] In addition to this, "a monthly living allowance while pursuing their studies," was appropriated as
well.[3]

The results of the program were astounding. "In the peak year of
1947, veterans accounted for 49 percent of college admissions. By the
time the original GI Bill ended on July 25, 1956, 7.8 million of the 16
million World War II veterans had participated in an education or training program."[4] This initial surge of college enrollment signifies the beginning of the modern higher education system.

Vastly different from the GI Bill fourteen years prior was the National Defense Education Act (NDEA) of 1958. Spurred out of panic
after the Soviet Union launched Sputniks I, II, and III between October 4, 1957, and May 15, 1958, Congress drafted a bill to counter the
emerging Soviet advancements in technology.[5]

> The Congress hereby finds and declares that the security of the
> Nation requires the fullest development of the mental resources and
> technical skills of its young men and women. The present emergency
> demands that additional and more adequate educational opportu-
> nities be made available. The defense of this Nation depends upon
> the mastery of modern techniques developed from complex scientif-
> ic principles. It depends as well upon the discovery and development
> of new principles, new techniques, and new knowledge.[6]

Although a majority of lawmakers had argued against giving college
students a "free ride" prior to the NDEA, legislators agreed that the
security of the nation trumped rhetorical partisan objections.[7] As a result, Congress committed to an initial eight-year program, starting at an
appropriation of $47 million for the fiscal year ending June 30, 1959.
Each year, the amount progressively rose until capping at $90 million
for the fiscal year ending June 30, 1962, and extending through the
fiscal year ending June 30, 1966.

This commitment eventually came to a total sum of $655 million in federal aid for loan assistance over this eight-year period.[8] Relative to CPI, this value would be equal to $5.2 billion today.[9] Such a significant investment in higher education was separated into loan amounts capped at $1,000 per fiscal year and $5,000 for all of the years enrolled.[10]

In order to fulfill the objective of promoting the sciences, "special consideration" was given to students "whose background indicate[d] a superior capacity or preparation in science, mathematics, engineering, or a modern foreign language."[11] As a result, the National Defense Education Act of 1958 stands as a milestone piece of legislation in developing the need for an organized student loan market.

Although the NDEA is overshadowed by the GI Bill and Higher Education Act (HEA), the NDEA was the first bill that proposed subsidizing higher education for the masses. In light of growing concerns over the Soviet Space Program and increasing competition in the international arena, its objectives were simple: strengthen the economy, improve innovation, and ensure national security. Higher education as it exists today rests upon this foundation, although one would not perceive it given the fundamental transformation that has occurred since this funding was installed in 1958.

The final piece of legislation came in 1965 with the Higher Education Act. Although the inevitable consequence of the HEA was to continue to build upon the legacy of sustaining technological innovation from the NDEA in 1958, the HEA was directed more toward a shifting set of cultural values that are most accurately characterized by President Lyndon Johnson's "Great Society Program."

In a speech delivered at the University of Michigan on May 22, 1964, President Johnson outlined his domestic agenda and ultimate vision of America. Education served as one of the three prongs to his approach in rebuilding the country. Highlighting the shortage of opportunity, he described how "each year more than 100,000 high school graduates with proved ability do not enter college because they cannot afford it," concluding that "poverty must not be a bar to learning, and learning must offer an escape from poverty."[12]

This rhetoric clearly demonstrates a shift in the attitude of American society relative to the outlook on higher education. This evolution began in 1944 with the GI Bill to help veterans of World War II to assimilate back into the American workforce. Then, with the NDEA in 1958, it shifted from a measure intended to help veterans, to promoting higher education to a broader base of potential applicants for national security reasons. Finally, in 1965 with the eventual signing of the HEA, this pool of included possible enrollees was expanded to virtually every-one, and viewed not as a privilege or something that was earned.

Rather, it was viewed as, and continues to be considered, an oppor-tunity that all Americans should have access to. As a consequence, enrollment rates soared in the years following its passage. With the market continuing to expand throughout the 1960s and into the early 1970s, there was a definitive need for an entity to establish order to a now vastly dynamic student lending industry.

Aside from the federal initiatives to increase college enrollment, there was also a growing social movement at the time of these pro-grams. Reflecting the sentiments of the HEA was a cultural paradigm shift that had been evolving over a twenty-year period following the conclusion of World War II. Prompting a new age of consumerism and the "American Dream" in the years following World War II, was the newfound realization of the average person that there was a vast world that existed beyond the borders of their small hometown communities.

Not only did the war physically remove young men and women from isolation during their military service, but also technological develop-ments throughout the period provided a spark for this phenomenon to continue, even after veterans returned home. Progress in technologies like the television, for example, quickly became an everyday household item that families enjoyed. Even more so than the earlier radio, televi-sion provided average Americans with a window to a vast world, other-wise blurred by the reality of daily seclusion.

"By the end of the decade, television was widely viewed as the me-dium of the future. After a promising start, RCA ran the first ad cam-paign for TV sets in 1940," and "became the first postwar manufacturer to advertise TV sets in 1946." During this time, "household penetration quickly rose from 0.5% in 1948 to more than one-third of homes in 1952."[13] This growing trend was further advanced when transcontinen-tal television services were first introduced with the AT&T airing of a presidential address by Harry S. Truman on September 4, 1951. For the first time, viewers from London to San Francisco tuned in to wit-ness the same broadcast at the same time.[14] This breakthrough serves as a microcosm for a world that was globalizing through a rapid period of growth in technological developments.

With this boom of innovation and economic prosperity came the explosion of consumerism and the American Dream. After having been exposed to the rest of world around them, former children of the Great Depression were now thirsty for an alternative to small-town life. The story of famed NASA engineer Homer Hickam illustrates this in the 1999 biographical film classic *October Sky*.[15]

The ambitious teenager from rural Coalwood, West Virginia, stands as a prime example for what many young men and women of his time experienced. Coming from a long line of coal miners, Homer, like many of his young counterparts in the late 1950s, wanted to do more than settle down to a forty-year career in the mines.

Looking to the famed scientist Warner von Braun as a symbol of inspiration, Homer graduated from high school in 1960. He then went on to attend Virginia Tech on a science scholarship that he earned after winning gold and silver in the area of "Propulsion" at the 1960 National Science Fair.[16] As the 1950s and 1960s wore on, this trend of young Americans taking advantage of federal initiatives to promote higher education advanced rapidly.

This twenty-year period, starting in 1944, stands as the beginning of the modern American higher education system that exists today. Three landmark pieces of legislation (GI Bill, 1944; NDEA, 1958; HEA, 1965) that were passed to achieve vastly different objectives were all related in working toward the common goal of extending higher education from the privileged sons of Wall Street to the humble children of Main Street.

By the time of the HEA passage in 1965, the cultural paradigm shift was finally being adopted and incorporated into legislation with the intent of creating an opportunity for all Americans to experience college training. This dual initiative from both Congress and everyday Americans led to an influx of college enrollment. In turn, this flood of new applicants eventually saturated the student loan market by the early 1970s.

As a result, Congress was obliged to create Sallie Mae, a government-sponsored enterprise (GSE), in 1972 as an entity to both facilitate and grow the booming industry of college loans. This is where our analysis of the student lending market begins.

ESSENTIAL TAKEAWAYS

Holding different objectives, three pieces of landmark legislation spanning from 1944 to 1965 represented the dawning of a new age in American higher education. Attempting to make college more affordable, the federal government opened access to millions of new students over the course of this twenty-year period.

Consistent with a shift in the cultural paradigm, young people looked to newly afforded college access as an opportunity to fulfill their dreams of seeing the world around them and entering careers that they were passionate about. Consequently, greater access from greater subsidies through grants and loans, combined with widespread enthusiasm to attend college, led to a booming of the college lending market. Ultimately, this would demand significant restructuring and support in the years ahead.

5

SALLIE MAE

The Rise of a Lending Empire

Sallie Mae has a long and complicated history spanning back to 1972. That year, the federal government sanctioned its creation as a government-sponsored enterprise (GSE) to provide funding for the newly established federal student loan program. A GSE is a federally chartered, privately owned, and privately controlled financial institution that lacks an express government guarantee, but benefits from the perception that the government stands behind its financial obligations.[1]

The Student Loan Marketing Association (Sallie Mae) was established as a "shareholder-owned, federally-chartered financial intermediary to provide financing and liquidity to the student loan market" through guaranteed loans under the Federal Family Education Loan Program (FFELP).[2] Over the course of a thirty-year period, Sallie Mae experienced much success in fulfilling its mission of expanding student lending volumes, providing reliable funding, and facilitating an active competition among a variety of institutions in the market.[3]

GSE lenders like Sallie Mae have served a vital role in achieving this end. Because "students rarely have an established credit record or sizeable assets," and instead have "little income, uncertain earnings prospects, 'unconventional' living arrangements, and a tendency to move frequently from one residence to another," commercial lenders often view college students as "an unattractive credit risk."[4] As a result, the demand for a lending firm to provide guaranteed loans to needy college students was crucial in continuing the legacy of the National Defense Education Act by facilitating and expanding financial accessibility to college.

First and foremost, much of the success that Sallie Mae had in penetrating the student loan market is largely attributed to the many privileges associated with the status of a GSE. Examples of government backing can be seen over the course of the company's first decade of operation as a start-up, when during this time the federal government granted Sallie Mae privileges that it did not extend to a majority of lenders.

A primary example of favorable treatment was special access to borrow through the Federal Financing Bank at minimal rates until September 30, 1984, at which time "the Department of Education could no longer guarantee Sallie Mae's debt."[5] Although Sallie Mae would not be able to borrow at reduced rates from the Federal Financing Bank after 1984, the Treasury Department offered a solution in allowing Sallie Mae loans to be adjusted at variable rates for up to fifteen-year terms, replacing one operating advantage with another.[6]

These early government supports accounted for 98 percent of Sallie Mae's resources,[7] permitting Sallie Mae to "leverage its small initial contribution of equity capital and quickly grow from a start-up company into a major financial institution."[8] The dramatic growth of Sallie Mae during this period is apparent in records released by the Congressional Budget Office (CBO), which indicate that Sallie Mae grew from $0.3 billion in assets in 1975 to $13.4 billion by 1985.[9]

While Sallie Mae enjoyed a series of tax benefits, regulatory exemptions, and reduced borrowing rates, there was a tradeoff to operating as a GSE. These compromises confine a GSE to a specified market niche with a limited range of services it is legally allowed to provide under the charter agreement.[10] For Sallie Mae, these limits manifested in the form of reducing its operating capacity to serving as a secondary market institution, in that "it could purchase loans that lenders originated, but could not itself originate loans."[11]

Consistent with the specified mission of Sallie Mae to *support* a competitive primary market by providing a source of funds for lenders as a secondary market entity, the company had virtually no ability to extend beyond its explicit mission of supplying loans to primary lenders. Although unsatisfied with these limits, which were viewed as an impediment to future growth capacity, Sallie Mae continued to take advantage of its charter benefits.

Strategically accepting securities exemptions from the SEC created significant borrowing power as a result of higher investment confidence with perceived government backing on obligations. Exploiting this bargaining power, Sallie Mae built itself into a market goliath, with lending assets accumulating to $39 billion by 1990.[12] By this time, not only did Sallie Mae hold the largest market share of guaranteed student loans, but its market share of 27 percent dwarfed its next largest competitor of Citibank, which held only 4 percent of the market share.[13]

A final indication of Sallie Mae's growth throughout the 1980s, and its intended growth over the course of the next decade, can be found in its investments in upgraded computerized management systems and operation support to improve the efficiency of processing student loans. Additionally, Sallie Mae also developed a state-of-the-art electronic communications system, enabling guarantors to receive, process, and return loan guarantees to lenders within twenty-four hours.[14]

Keep in mind, had it not been for the perceived government guarantee as a GSE, allowing Sallie Mae to operate at much lower costs than their competitors, many of the investments that were central to Sallie Mae's growth would not have been feasible. This, in turn, enabled Sallie

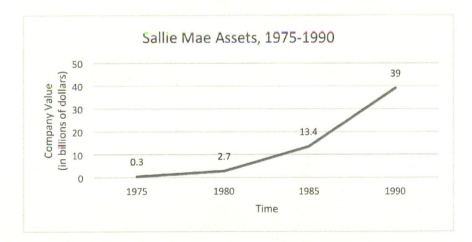

Figure 5.1.   Growth of Sallie Mae as a GSE, 1975–1990. *Source: Thomas H. Stanton, "The Privatization of Sallie Mae and Its Consequences," p. 9, figure 3, "Growth of Sallie Mae as a GSE, 1975–1995."*

Mae to make large financial investments in servicing student loans and educational facilities obligations as a secondary market entity. Leading the industry in commercial and technological investment, Sallie Mae was quickly catapulted to being the dominant market firm for student loans, eager to expand its empire.

Postured as a formidable force in a booming student loan market, Sallie Mae was now equipped and eager to expand upon its role in the industry, but could not do so until its GSE charter with the federal government was severed. Sallie Mae primarily hoped to expand into loan origination, where a majority of the money can potentially be made in the lending process.

As a private firm, Sallie Mae would be able to originate loans on its own without having to purchase them from other lenders, as stipulated under the GSE charter agreement. Having the ability to individually purchase loans would grant Sallie Mae more power to negotiate, as it could threaten to directly compete in the bank's market unless the bank agreed to terms that were favorable to Sallie Mae.[15]

In addition to loan origination, Sallie Mae also had aspirations of increasing share value for investors through revenue diversification, by means of investing in areas completely unrelated to the charter mission as a firm assigned to the secondary student loan market, such as health-care. Until they could convince the federal government to remove their GSE status, Sallie Mae was significantly limited in their ability to generate revenue, relative to their potential.

Although the promise of greater economic return was enough to encourage Sallie Mae to eventually privatize, an emerging wave of government regulation would soon turn the privatization of Sallie Mae from a move of strategic benefit to one of necessity. Spurred largely from the fallout of the savings and loan crisis,[16] Congress became concerned with the risks associated with GSEs, including Sallie Mae, by the late 1980s. This quickly prompted the Treasury Department, CBO, and GAO to file reports on these potential liabilities, making recommendations that would heighten oversight and thereby reduce risk to the government.

These measures included regular risk assessments of Sallie Mae that would be filed independently by each of the three overseeing bodies, as well as subjecting Sallie Mae to the oversight of a new centralized supervising agency that would be in charge of monitoring all GSEs.[17]

This meant that Sallie Mae would be required to disclose all records on systems and personnel, internal controls, financial performance, and business strategies.[18]

To no surprise, Sallie Mae fiercely opposed these recommendations, saying that increased regulation would "stifle creativity and impede the ability of Sallie Mae to manage its risk and quickly and creatively respond to programmatic initiatives requested or supported by our congressional overseers."[19] With the limits on potential economic gains compounded with the wave of recommended oversight and scrutiny as a GSE, Sallie Mae vigorously launched a series of negotiations to sever its charter with the federal government.[20]

While Sallie Mae scrambled to launch a privatization campaign, reports from the Treasury, CBO, and GAO continued to clamor for increased oversight of Sallie Mae. Responding to their findings, Congress began implementing reforms to correct some of these problems. The first can be seen with the Credit Reform Act of 1990, which instituted new budget rules for federal student loans and other credit programs. Until the enactment of credit reform, credit program costs were accounted for on a cash basis, meaning that the budget "overstated the costs of direct loans, which involved immediate cash outlays, and understated the costs of guaranteed loans, which cost the government money only as a loan defaulted and the government paid the claim."[21]

The reformed accounting procedure for credit programs consists of estimating the net value of the future costs relative to revenues that the government will receive from all of the federal loans originated in a single year. This new assessment criteria eliminated the artificial budget scoring advantages of federal guaranteed loans, while highlighting direct student loans as an attractive alternative.

Although the Credit Reform Act of 1990 was significant in its short-term corrections to the student loan market, its long-term effects were even more important. With direct loans now standing as an appealing alternative to guaranteed loans, Congress supported the creation of a five-year pilot "Direct Loan Program" in the 1992 amendments to the Higher Education Act, which President George H. W. Bush signed into law.

With this, power was given to the Department of Education to make student loans directly to students, which now stood in direct competition with guaranteed student loans, such as those serviced by Sallie Mae under FFELP.[22] During the first year of this pilot program, Sallie Mae's stock price fell by 40 percent, dropping the market value of the company by over $2.5 billion through the next year.[23]

Understanding the significant influence that this pilot program had on its narrowly chartered business model and stock valuation as a result, Sallie Mae feared the prospect of the five-year pilot program becoming a permanent threat. This fear became a reality with the election of President Bill Clinton, who supported a fundamental transformation of federal student lending programs throughout his two terms as president.

The first of these policies implemented under the Clinton Administration was the Student Loan Reform Act of 1993, which signified a new and combative relationship between the federal government and Sallie Mae. Most indicative of this fact was an "offset fee" of 0.30 percent, applied exclusively to Sallie Mae on federally guaranteed student loans that it acquired after August 10, 1993.[24] This revenue would be used to fund other lending programs in order to "offset" the advantages that Sallie Mae enjoyed as a GSE in the guaranteed student loan market.

Additional constraints included a lender-paid origination fee, a decline in government's coverage of credit defaults, and a reduction to loan generation.[25] However, the most damaging effect to Sallie Mae from the Student Loan Reform Act of 1993 was the adoption of the Federal Direct Lending Program (FDLP) as a permanent program, with plans to dramatically expand its role in the student loan market.

Direct loans were viewed as a way to significantly simplify the student lending process. While the FFELP delivery system of loans involved "five kinds of loans, more than 7,500 educational institutions, about 7,800 commercial lenders, 35 secondary marketers, and 46 state or nonprofit agencies," the Department of Education would make loans directly to students.[26] This transition phased out the need for commercial lenders, guaranty agencies, and secondary markets, eliminating costs such as interest payments made to lenders while students attend college, as well as special allowance payments to lenders meant to subsidize the yield on student loans.[27]

In order to achieve this, the Treasury Department would raise loan capital by issuing securities, which the Department of Education would then use to service and collect the loans.[28] As a result, Sallie Mae help-

lessly watched its stock valuation continue to plummet, as the company
lost over $4 billion in shareholder value between February 1993 and
June 1995.[29] The future survival of Sallie Mae hinged on a single factor.
If the federal government decided to convert all of its loans from
FFELP to the FDLP, the best option left for Sallie Mae would be to
"liquidate its franchise."[30] Consequently, the fate of Sallie Mae would
be decided over the course of the next three years.

At this point in time, it was mutually beneficial for both Sallie Mae
and the federal government to permit and facilitate Sallie Mae's full
privatization. From the standpoint of the government, privatizing Sallie
Mae worked to "ensure a smooth transition from guaranteed loans
under FFELP to direct loans under the FDLP."[31]

Additionally, falling stock prices at Sallie Mae, almost entirely
caused by the emergence of the FDLP, posed a serious liability to the
federal government. If Sallie Mae became insolvent, the federal
government would have no choice but to make good on Sallie Mae's
financial obligations, as it was the single largest servicer of guaranteed
student loans in the country.

In regard to the incentives for Sallie Mae to privatize, the political
risk, the offset fee, and the threat of more regulation had become so
great that having to liquidate the company was a very real possibility if it
did not succeed in its objective to privatize.[32] Making the case to reorganize and relinquish its GSE status, Sallie Mae insisted that the mission of its charter had been fulfilled:

> In creating the various GSEs, Congress did not contemplate the
> need at some point to unwind or terminate their federal charters.
> However, Congress did not assume the perpetual existence (and
> continual expansion) of individual GSEs in the context of changing
> social and economic priorities. The missing element in the GSE con-
> cept is the notion of a life cycle for government sponsorship. GSEs
> are created to increase the flow of funds to socially desirable activ-
> ities. If successful, they grow and mature as the market develops. At
> some point, the private sector may be able to meet the funding needs
> of the particular market segment. If so, a sunset may be appropri-
> ate.[33]

Emphasizing this point, Sallie Mae presented its privatization proposal
to lawmakers soon after.

Following three years of heated negotiations, Congress enacted the Student Loan Marketing Association Reorganization Act of 1996, setting a course for Sallie Mae's gradual yet complete privatization by December 29, 2004.[34] It is from this series of negotiations that Sallie Mae leveraged enough flexibility and resources to build upon the unprecedented level of growth that continues even today, twenty years later.

Over the course of the next three years, a series of turbulent negotiations were conducted between Sallie Mae, Congress, and relevant executive branch agencies. The focus of early proposals for privatization revolved around a concern of Sallie Mae's size.

Fearing that Sallie Mae was "too big to fail," even as a private firm, the CBO proposed to "divide the firm into several independent entities and require Sallie Mae to divest itself gradually by disturbing shares in each of the newly created private firms to its existing shareholders"[35] under the AT&T breakup model.[36] Small enough to avoid "too big to fail" status, these entities would be free of an implied guarantee, eliminating the threat of a bailout altogether.

Opposed to the limits associated with a corporate division, Sallie Mae insisted that the AT&T breakup model was not an appropriate standard for this case. Highlighting the differences between Sallie Mae and AT&T, Sallie Mae executives suggested that while AT&T was a monopoly over the single market of local telephone service, Sallie Mae was engaged in "two highly competitive markets, financial services and transaction processing, where there were no fixed cost barriers to entry."[37]

Additionally, Sallie Mae also objected to early proposals of an "exit fee" that would "reorganize the benefits Sallie Mae had received because of its GSE status . . . including low borrowing rates, better financial leverage than private institutions, and exemption from state and local taxes."[38]

As pressure mounted to constrain Sallie Mae's privatization by assessing harsh exit fees and breaking it into small entities with limited capacities thereafter, Sallie Mae developed the concept of a holding company with several operating subsidiaries.[39] Over an established transition period, the holding company would oversee existing portfolios under the GSE, but would begin any additional portfolios under the newly established private operating subsidiaries of the holding company.[40] However, during this transition period, the GSE would retain limited benefits, including exemption from state qualification requirements, exemption from anti-trust laws, and tax credits for financing underserved markets.[41]

Additionally, GSE shareholders would be entitled to vote on a plan for privatization, developed by the board of executives, which, if privatized reorganization was not supported by a majority of its stockholders, would result in its liquidation completely. Upon the likelihood of shareholders voting to reorganize rather than liquidate, investors would then have the ability to exchange their GSE shares for shares of the holding company.[42]

Over time, the GSE assets would eventually shift to the private operating subsidiaries of the Sallie Mae holding company until the GSE was liquidated, which would then signal the end of the transition period and classify Sallie Mae as an exclusively private firm.

Following the series of testimonies and proposals from executive agencies and Sallie Mae officials, Rep. Howard "Buck" McKeon introduced a bill to privatize Sallie Mae on May 11, 1995. Favoring Sallie Mae, the bill adopted many of the proposals laid out by Sallie Mae, such as adopting the holding company concept over the CBO's AT&T break-up model and initially limited oversight from the Treasury, against the Treasury's recommendations.[43]

The bill also demonstrated a significant shift in assessed fees. Failing to adopt a proposal that applied a $535 million exit fee, intended to compensate for years of financial benefits, the bill transitioned to a focus on budget neutrality that applied more modest offset fees.[44]

Soon after, the Clinton Administration responded to the proposed bill by sending Deputy Assistant Treasury Secretary Darcy Brown to testify before the Senate. During these hearings, Ms. Brown demanded greater "safety and soundness oversight powers" over Sallie Mae, in requiring approval from the Treasury and Education departments before a reorganization plan could be adopted by Sallie Mae, as well as placing GSE operations under heightened oversight until liquidation.[45]

After the Clinton Administration had completed its testimony of recommendations for the bill, a series of legislative maneuvers[46] were followed with the bill's passage in the House of Representatives on September 28, 1996.[47] Two days later, the bill passed in the Senate and the president signed the Student Loan Marketing Association Reorganization Act of 1996 into law on September 30, 1996.[48] Operating as law, the act amended section 439 of the Higher Education Act of 1965, adding the new section of 440 that outlined the options for the future of Sallie Mae.[49]

In the most basic of terms, the Student Loan Marketing Association Reorganization Act, under section 440 of the HEA, established two alternatives to facilitate the complete dissolution of Sallie Mae. The first option "required Sallie Mae to propose a plan of reorganization to its shareholders under which their shares would convert to equal shares in a new state-chartered holding company."[50] If the plan was approved by its shareholders, Sallie Mae would be reorganized during a "wind-down" period, during which the GSE would be gradually "phased out by September 30, 2008."[51]

The contingent plan was also established under section 440 as a sunset provision of the legislation, which would be activated in the event that the shareholders rejected the plan, causing the GSE to be liquidated by July 1, 2013, without a holding company or its subsidiaries to replace it.[52] Voting overwhelmingly in favor of reorganization on July 31, 1997, the sunset provisions of the contingent liquidation plan were null and void, activating the reorganization provisions under section 440.

"Pursuant to the Privatization Act, a Delaware-chartered corpora-tion, SLM Corporation, ultimately became the parent company of Sallie Mae," under which all Sallie Mae employees and property were trans-ferred to the holding company "as soon as practicable"[53] during reor-ganization.[54]

Although SLM Corporation was restricted from using the "Sallie Mae" name as an issuer of debt obligation and bound to disclosure requirements until three years after the dissolution date, SLM Corpora-tion was permitted to purchase the "Sallie Mae" name as a "trademark or service mark" for the amount of $5 million.[55] Having done so, both the private holding company and its subsidiaries, as well as the dimin-ishing GSE, were all able to use the Sallie Mae name in almost every aspect of business.

While the private subsidiaries and the GSE may have been linked in name, section 440 made sure to create strict firewalls between the two. While the GSE continued to "have all of the rights, privileges, and obligations set forth in section 439 . . . the holding company and any subsidiary of the holding company [was] not entitled to any of the rights, privileges, and obligations" of the GSE.[56] These restrictions allowed for the company to unite under a single name of Sallie Mae, while preserving the benefits of the GSE to function at lower operating costs under its charter, but preventing the private subsidiaries from abusing these accommodations.

While retaining the Sallie Mae brand name and GSE charter benefits were victories for the firm, Sallie Mae also experienced several punitive losses, largely as a result of recommendations made by the Clinton Administration through the testimony of Darcy Bradbury.[57] Under section 440(8), Congress increased the Treasury's authority to enforce the GSE to "obtain, maintain, and report information," in that the Treasury Secretary is issued the right to make inquiries on "(i) the financial risk to the Association . . . to the extent such activities are reasonably likely to have a material impact on the financial condition of the Association, and (ii) the Association's policies, procedures, and systems for monitoring and controlling any such financial risk."[58] These provisions also gave the Treasury the authority to make inquiries regarding financial risk posed by "associated persons," which extended coverage beyond GSE personnel to its private subsidiary affiliates.[59]

Along with the increase in Treasury oversight, Sallie Mae was also obligated to engage in several financial transactions with the DC Financial Control Board, under section 440(9). While Sallie Mae managed to avoid an express exit fee, it effectively paid a total of $42 million in offset fees to the DC Financial Control Board for DC Public Schools.[60]

In addition to these fees, section 440 also required Sallie Mae to issue warrants to the DC Financial Control Board "equal to 1% of its outstanding shares that could be exercised to purchase stock of the holding company at any time prior to September 30, 2008."[61] From this agreement, the DC Financial Control Board received $37 million upon the sale of these SLM Corporation common stock warrants.[62]

A final provision of section 440 consisted of a mechanism that would wind down the GSE's remaining debt obligations after its dissolution date on September 30, 2008. Known as defeasance, "the organization irrevocably transferred sufficient funds or Treasury obligations to a trust and, under the trust agreement, assured that the trustee would make full repayment of all liabilities on outstanding GSE obligations."[63]

In essence, Sallie Mae would be responsible for fulfilling all of its GSE obligations, even after the GSE was dissolved. Agreeing to these terms, shareholders practically voted unanimously to adopt the reorganization plan, established under the guidelines of section 440 of the Higher Education Act. The vote quickly moved Sallie Mae forward on a path to privatization over a transition period that would begin on July 31, 1997, and end on December 29, 2004.

While at the surface, Sallie Mae appeared united in a common objective to reorganize under the agreed-upon plan for privatization, an internal dispute between shareholders suggested a far different reality. Throughout the course of the negotiations leading up to privatization, an internal power struggle within Sallie Mae had thoroughly developed. The two sides consisted of one group of directors who backed the existing management that headed negotiations during this period, and an opposing group of directors called the Committee to Restore Value (CRV), who believed the company was moving in the wrong direction under the persisting negotiations.

Tensions escalated when CRV supporters succeeded in contesting sitting directors of existing management for their seats during board elections in 1995. Prior to privatization, the Higher Education Act "required that Sallie Mae's board of directors be composed of 21 persons, 7 appointed by the President of the United States, and 14 selected by shareholders."[64] Largely as a consequence of shareholder discontent over the decline of Sallie Mae's stock, the CRV gained control of eight of the twenty-one seats in the aftermath of the 1995 board elections, constituting a majority support from shareholder-elected seats.[65]

At this same time, however, the negotiations stage of privatization was virtually over with the drafting of legislation already underway. Consequently, Sallie Mae's proposals were only reflective of thirteen directors, who favored the strategy of continuing to operate primarily as a secondary market role that "partnered" with banks, while also diversifying its revenue through expanding servicing options, consulting, and other technology-oriented subsidiaries.[66]

This effectively disenfranchised the eight newly elected board members who represented the CRV's more aggressive strategy of shifting the company to a direct origination model that would compete with banks and other lenders for loans in the primary market, while also applying the diversification of revenue sources through fee services that were consistent with existing management's proposals.[67] Quite simply, the two combating factions within Sallie Mae had many of the same proposals, but emphasized different sections.

Existing management wanted to cautiously venture into loan origination as a support for the larger business model, centered as a secondary market entity with a focus on expanding servicing options and technology that partnered with banks. Contrarily, CRV members hoped to aggressively pursue loan origination as a direct competitor with banks, using service and technology fee diversification as the support to the loan origination core of the business model.

With the signing of the Student Loan Marketing Association Reorganization Act into law on September 30, 1996, Sallie Mae's board was faced with the task of voting upon its plan for reorganization, which would ultimately set the course for the company's future. Recognizing the significance of this vote, both groups saw it "as an opportunity to solidify (in the case of management) or seize (in the case of the CRV) control over the board directors and the future of the company."[68]

Following several months of debate and posturing, the board of directors adopted the management's plan for reorganization on January 24, 1997, by a thirteen-to-eight vote, with the eight CRV representatives voting unanimously against the plan.[69] In addition to the existing management's victory of initially passing a reorganization plan that favored their interests, the plan also seemingly secured this path for the company in future years with an election process that created a "slate of directors that would have greatly weakened, if not eliminated, the CRV dissenters."[70]

In response to management offering two seats to CRV affiliates on the condition that they refrain from voicing public dissent to the reorganization plan, both CRV directors withdrew their names from the management slate in February 1997, and began a movement to bring the matter "directly to shareholders."[71]

Following several months of contentious debate and realignment among key shareholders, the CRV ultimately received 58 percent of the shareholder vote at the final meeting on July 31, 1997, placing the CRV slate of directors in control of the company.[72] In August, the company was reorganized, with the SLM Corporation holding company overseeing its private and GSE subsidiaries.

Additionally, "Albert Lord was installed as the CEO and vice chairman of the holding company," while Edward Fox, Sallie Mae's first CEO, who had retired in 1990, "assumed the position of Chairman of the Board under the CRV slate," where the two served in these positions over the entire transition period.[73] After years of negotiation, the vision of a Sallie Mae loaning empire could finally become a reality.

ESSENTIAL TAKEAWAYS

Established as a GSE to support the growing student lending market under the charter as secondary market lender, Sallie Mae was established in 1972. Granted special operating conditions, Sallie Mae enjoyed significant market benefits that allowed it to overrun competitors and establish itself as a formidable lending giant by the early 1990s.

Having leveraged enough power to thrive without GSE charter protections and limited by the charter conditions, Sallie Mae lobbied for privatization. In the wake of increased regulation and scrutiny of GSEs following the savings and loan crisis, these efforts were enhanced as privatization moved from a point of opportunity to necessity.

Following a three-year-long negotiation process, Sallie Mae was able to construct a privatization plan with several key operating advantages that would propel it not only into privatization but also as an entity with market control over the industry. Exploiting these terms of the agreement under a new CRV faction of the board and shareholders that overtook Sallie Mae upon the conclusion of the negotiations, the new SLM Corporation had postured itself in ways that would solidify its dominance over the student lending market.

6

RIGGED

Before venturing into the details of the transition period and beyond, it is important to reflect upon the significance of the power transfer within Sallie Mae during the summer of 1997. Set on the course of a limited primary market presence and a focus on service and technology fee operations, early management exclusively negotiated with Congress and relative administrative agencies in the years leading up to the privatization of Sallie Mae.

Following the assurance from Sallie Mae executives throughout these negotiations that a private Sallie Mae would largely avoid the primary market of loan origination, the Student Loan Marketing Association Reorganization Act was signed into law in the fall of 1996, in the good faith that Sallie Mae would fulfill its promises. Within a year's time, however, the very management that agreed to such terms was replaced by the CRV, a group of Sallie Mae renegades, adamant on a course of intrusive expansion into the primary lending market and beyond.

This begs the question: If Congress knew that such a transfer of power was to take place, would it have manufactured a bill with provisions such as a generously long transition period, GSE retention of charter benefits, the exclusion of heavy exit fees, and the opportunity to buy the Sallie Mae name at a minimal price, all intended to assist SLM Corporation through the process? Although we will never surely know the answer to this question, it is reasonable to speculate that Congress would be more likely to grant a non-threatening support to the industry (early management's plan) with certain privileges, that it might not otherwise offer to an aggressive corporate machine determined on a path for market dominance (CRV's plan).

Due to the order in the sequence of events, Sallie Mae essentially pulled an unintended and unanticipated bait and switch on Congress. While the industry-support advocates of early management negotiated the terms of the Student Loan Marketing Association Reorganization Act, it was the CRV board of dominance-driven directors that ultimately inherited, and arguably abused, a law that was created from earlier negotiations they were not even a part of. The consequences of this were apparent throughout its transition period to privatization, with lasting effects that continue to unravel even today.

Between 1997 and 2006, Sallie Mae's portfolio of managed student loans increased from $43.7 billion to $142.1 billion, signifying a 325 percent increase.[1] Continuing to practice its use of "technology and economies of scale in servicing" to achieve lower operation costs, Sallie Mae was able to expand exponentially without the interference of narrow charter limits.[2]

Additionally, Sallie Mae has also tested restrictions imposed upon the company by laws and regulations as a way to gain an advantage in the market. This has become apparent in the area of "opportunity pools," with the creation of Sallie Mae's Opportunity Loan Program in 2001. Under the program, "Sallie Mae provides private (i.e., nonfederal) loans to colleges that the colleges can lend to students without an established credit history or with past credit problems who otherwise might not qualify for a private loan."[3]

As compensation for taking on particularly high-risk portfolios, Sallie Mae restricts schools affiliated with the program to using Sallie Mae as its exclusive lender under the contract, which is wielded as a tool to quickly drive out competition on an institutional basis. Speaking to this point, Suzanne Mettler explains that Sallie Mae "possessed the resources and expertise to market their services to universities and colleges," providing "financial incentives for universities to endorse them as their 'preferred lenders,' offering kickbacks and other incentives in exchange for help in channeling students their way."[4]

Along these same lines, Sallie Mae has also significantly added to its lobbying capacity, resulting in $13 million to finance its lobbying operation between 1997 and 2003.[5] This has "placed the company third within the credit industry on lobbying expenditures," further expanding its competitive edge into the political arena.[6]

In conjunction with each of these growth methods, Sallie Mae was also successful in adopting the concept of and developing the market for asset-backed securities. "Asset-backed securities (ABS) are created by bundling assets, such as student loans, into pools and establishing trusts, which then issue securities backed by the cash flows from a pool of loans sold to the trust."[7] After completing its first ABS transaction in October 1995, "Sallie Mae developed its capacity to work with the rating agencies and the U.S. Securities and Exchange Commission. Sallie Mae's size, name recognition, and efficiency provided advantages over its smaller competitors," leading to the issuance of $120 billion in ABS over the remaining transition period.[8]

While economies of scale, opportunity pools, lobbying expenditures, and asset-backed securities have all contributed in some significant way to the expansion of Sallie Mae and the evolution of the market, it is Sallie Mae's influence on the 1998 and 2005 amendments to the Higher Education Act that have had the most profound and long-lasting effects on the industry.

Of the $13 million spent on lobbying between 1997 and 2003, House Speaker John Boehner and Rep. Howard "Buck" McKeon have been the top two beneficiaries of SLM Corp. contributions, at $259,720 and $233,000.[9] Coincidentally, Rep. McKeon not only sponsored the initial Student Loan Marketing Association Reorganization Act of 1996, allowing Sallie Mae to privatize in the first place, but also introduced the 1998 amendments to the Higher Education Act as a seasoned member of the House Committee on Education and the Workforce.[10]

These amendments effectively required the debtor to "demonstrate 'undue hardship' no matter how long ago the student debts were incurred," striking the provision that allowed education loans to be discharged after seven years in repayment and significantly reducing the market risk of student loans discharging through bankruptcy.[11]

As for then-representative Boehner, his support as the chairman of the House Committee on Education and the Workforce between 2001 and 2006 proved to be a helpful asset for Sallie Mae throughout this transition period, particularly in the case of additional amendments that were added to the HEA in 2005.[12] The importance of the 2005 amendments is reflected in Sallie Mae's particularly high level of campaign contributions in the 2004 election cycle, spending a total of $1.475 million.[13]

The 2005 amendments were particularly significant in that restrictions on dischargability of student loans were extended entirely to private loans, applying all loans to the "undue hardship" standard.[14] Reducing the likelihood that student loans will be discharged in bankruptcy alleviates an incredible amount of risk on behalf of the lender, in that restricting access to discharge for student borrowers insulates lenders from potential loss and reduces the incentives of the lender to monitor borrowers and ration credit.[15]

Thus, tuition prices have skyrocketed over the last decade, because lenders are virtually free of all risk limits in lending, leaving them the capacity to lend out large sums of money to people who would not otherwise qualify in a market where significant risk exists. With colleges free to compete on perks and prestige while virtually ignoring costs, and lenders obliged to respond to higher tuition rates with larger loans and higher returns on interest as a result, colleges now have the capacity to continue raising tuition rates at unprecedented levels.

In essence, the 1998 and 2005 amendments, sponsored and supported by the two highest beneficiaries of SLM Corp. campaign contributions, have orchestrated a student lending market that is rigged in favor of prestige-obsessed colleges and profit-seeking lenders, all at the expense of the student.

With the market securely rigged in favor of lenders, Sallie Mae embarked on a series of horizontal and vertical acquisitions, buying up regional competitors across the country in the following year. Starting in the northeast, Sallie Mae began this mission with the purchase of Nellie Mae, "a large New England lender with a $2.6 billion student loan portfolio."[16]

Soon after, Sallie Mae expanded west and south, first acquiring Student Loan Funding Resources, a large Cincinnati lender with a $3 billion portfolio, as well as "entering an exclusive relationship with Chase Manhattan Bank to purchase all student loans originated by Chase," amounting to $5 billion in additional portfolios in 1999.[17]

"Stunning the student loan industry," Sallie Mae went on to acquire USA Group Inc., the nation's largest student loan guaranty agency in guarantee servicing, student loan servicing, and secondary market operation.[18] This particular acquisition was key to future expansion, in that it allowed the company "to provide a full spectrum of administrative support services to loan guarantors, ranging from loan origination and account maintenance to default prevention and post-default collections."[19] The acquisition also gained "guarantor servicing contracts with guarantors serving 12 other states," and provided Sallie Mae a "stream of fee income from the provision of delinquency and default management services primarily to guaranty agencies."[20]

Additionally, Sallie Mae also sought to acquire Noel-Levitz, one of the nation's leading "enrollment-management" consulting companies in the practice of "financial-aid leveraging,"[21] assisting more than 1,600 colleges and universities since 1973.[22] By the end of FY 2000, Sallie Mae served approximately 5,500 financial institutions and state agencies, as well as over 7 million student loan borrowers, ultimately servicing $66.7 billion in FFELP loans and $5.8 billion in non-FFELP loans.[23]

Catapulting from the USA Group Inc. and Noel-Levitz acquisitions, Sallie Mae spent the following four years infiltrating practically every aspect of the student loan market in virtually every corner of the country.

Continuing upon its vertical expansion in the market, Sallie Mae moved into the student loan collection business through two acquisitions, the first being Pioneer Credit Recovery Inc., "one of the largest loan collection companies for the Department of Education," and the other being General Revenue Corporation, "one of the largest school-focused collection companies."[24]

In 2003, Sallie Mae shifted the company's focus to its "relationships with schools' bursars and business offices," acquiring a large FFELP lender and leading provider of tuition payment plans, Academic Management Services Corp. (AMS).[25] "AMS is the leading provider of tuition payment plans, with more than 550 colleges and universities using AMS's products," and has "developed strong relationships with schools' bursars and business offices."[26]

Following the AMS acquisition in 2003, Sallie Mae purchased Southwest Student Services Corporation, which targeted Arizona and Florida markets, as well as the Student Loan Finance Association, directly exposing the remaining northwest market to Sallie Mae by the end of 2004.[27] As Sallie Mae suggested, "With a vast array of products and service offerings, we are positioned to meet the growing demand for post-secondary education credit and related services," employing over nine thousand employees by the end of 2004.[28]

As Sallie Mae continued to expand through a series of horizontal and vertical acquisitions, shareholder returns on common equity[29] suggested that a growth strategy based upon buying out regional competition was working. Increasing from a 30 percent return in 2001, still relatively high compared to other major lenders, returns on common equity sharply rose to 73 percent by 2004, largely as a result of the firm's reaction to increased assets and less competition.[30]

Taking an advantage of a long transition period that lasted between 1997 and 2004, Sallie Mae succeeded in increasing its market share significantly through this series of acquisitions in the education finance market. From the "dominant position that the company had built as a GSE through servicing economies of scale, technology platforms, and relations with schools," Sallie Mae had grown to a corporate structure consisting of seven education credit agencies, two education savings firms, two consumer credit partnerships, two acquisition and funding entities, three servicing organizations, a default aversion group, and four collection agencies.[31]

Although each of these acquisitions is significant in its own way, Sallie Mae would not be what it currently is today without its purchase of an industrial bank charter, approved by the Utah Department of Financial Institutions in 2005, which began funding and originating student loans by 2006 through the Sallie Mae Bank.[32]

As a vital part of the company's vertical integration strategy, its industrial bank allows the company to "expand the range of products and services that it offers," originating $1.6 billion in mortgages and consumer loans in 2006 alone.[33] Additional financial advantages of operating an industrial bank, such as accessing reduced processing charges through the Federal Reserve payment system, have further enabled Sallie Mae to expand significantly.

From its $122 billion in student loan assets, which accounted for 27 percent of federal student loan origination in 2005, Sallie Mae quickly grew to controlling over one-third of the market share by 2012.[34] However, Sallie Mae did not simply rely on the benefits of operating its own bank to expand.

Continuing to service loans originated by FFELP through July 1, 2010, Sallie Mae has also secured an $8.5 billion line of credit at an initial rate of 0.23 percent interest from the Federal Home Loan Bank (FHLB).[35] Sallie Mae then converts this revenue into fixed-rate student loans, which it then charges borrowers rates of interest that are 25–40 times higher than the rate they originally borrowed from through the FHLB.[36]

The combination of access to low-cost secured borrowings and charging significantly higher interest rates to students has led to a profit of "$2.5 billion in interest income from its private student loan business."[37] Ironically, this arrangement with the FHLB, which holds a GSE mission to increase access to home-ownership, has actually reduced the affordability of home-ownership to students as a result of high-interest private student loans that are issued by Sallie Mae.[38]

With the average student loan burden spiking by nearly 15 percent between 2007 and 2010, partly attributed to high-interest private loans, the number of Americans ages 25 to 34 living with their parents experienced a sharp increase from 4.7 million in 2007 to nearly 6 million by 2011.[39]

Despite significant market gains as a result of the Sallie Mae–FHLB partnership in 2010, Sallie Mae did not experience its single largest

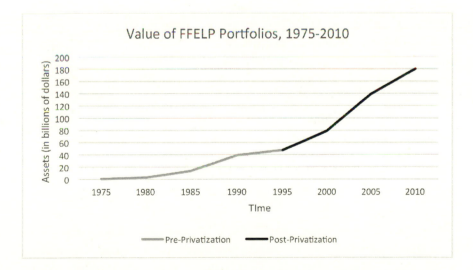

Figure 6.1.   Sallie Mae Growth Since Privatization.   *Source: Thomas H. Stanton, "The Privatization of Sallie Mae and Its Consequences," p. 18, figure 4: "Total Student Loan Dollars."*

market gain until a recent corporate restructuring in 2013. This restructuring occurred when Sallie Mae split itself into two publicly traded companies.

The first entity consists of an education loans management firm that "will focus on servicing federal student loans."[40] This branch of Sallie Mae owns approximately "95 percent of Sallie Mae's assets, including about $118.1 billion in old FFELP loans."[41] When combined with other past private portfolios and additional assets, this division was worth approximately $168.4 billion in 2013.[42]

The other firm includes a consumer banking business that handles "all private loan origination and services including Sallie Mae Bank loans,"[43] equating to approximately $9.9 billion in assets that are intended to "concentrate on the fast-growing business of making private loans."[44] By doing so, Sallie Mae is effectively "splitting off the higher-risk profile business" from the "steady cash flow business."[45]

This has ultimately exposed Sallie Mae to a "new set of investors" that are "more comfortable paying a higher multiple[46] for a bank with a small base of high-quality loans that will grow at a rapid clip."[47] Separated from the large pool of guaranteed FFELP loans that are serviced by Sallie Mae, the Sallie Mae Bank now has the capacity to cater to the interests of these new investors by expanding upon private loans that can "refuse to lend to less credit-worthy borrowers or charge higher rates to compensate for the risk."[48]

Looking forward, this restructuring is intended to transform the company in a way that phases out the old model of servicing FFELP loans through the federal government, shifting the focus toward an emerging private student loan market. Consequently, Sallie Mae recorded $4 billion in originated private loans the following year, "almost twice its 2010 lending level,"[49] catapulting Sallie Mae from a 32 percent market share to 51 percent in a single year.[50]

Additionally, Sallie Mae's stock valuation has also benefited substantially as a result of the recent growth induced by the corporate restructuring. From the 2012 year-end stock value of $17.13, Sallie Mae's stock spiked to $26.28 by the end of 2013.[51] Given the company's recent growth and position as the dominant firm in private loan origination, Sallie Mae has secured its place as the preeminent power in the student lending market.

Over the last several years, Sallie Mae's increasing corporate returns to shareholders is not the only trend the firm has established. Amid rising concern over growing debt burdens on students, the Consumer Financial Protection Bureau (CFPB) began accepting private student loan complaints in March 2012, from which a series of reports were filed that detailed many of the market abuses.

In a second wave of 3,800 additional complaints that were submitted between October 1, 2012, and September 30, 2013, the Annual Report of the CFPB Student Loan Ombudsman "offers analysis, commentary, and recommendations to address issues reported by consumers in the student loan marketplace."[52] Of the 3,800 complaints filed during this period of time, 49 percent came from students who had loans being serviced by Sallie Mae.[53]

While the most common complaints surrounded cases of "borrowers attempting to adjust the repayment terms of their loans in times of hardship," additional problems concerning "debt collection practices, payment processing issues, and general customer service" were among the most reported offenses.[54]

In respect to payment-processing problems, complications begin with the interest rates accruing daily on student loans, resulting in a total bill that depends on when the payment is submitted. As the report suggests, "there is significant confusion about payment policies with regard to 'paid ahead' or 'advanced payment' status. Borrowers note that after submitting additional payments, they were placed in 'paid ahead' or 'advanced payment' status."[55] This makes it unclear "whether funds have been held in order to satisfy a future payment or whether the servicer has actually applied the payment toward the principal balance."[56]

Such confusion is significant in that if the consumer "remits a payment to satisfy a full future installment, the next billing statement may reflect a $0.00 payment . . . leading many to be unsure as to whether their automatic debit payment will be processed or if they need to submit a payment the following month."[57]

Adding further confusion, it is common for student loan borrowers to take out multiple loans, often "bundled into a single account ('billing group')" that, despite being managed from a single loan servicer, carries with it several "different balances, different interest rates, and different amortization schedules," further complicating how to apply payments that minimize the overall cost.[58]

The report goes on to provide a hypothetical student loan borrower with three loans, each with a balance of $10,000, but having different interest rates of 7, 9, and 13 percent. With a minimum monthly payment of $400, the borrower could expect to pay the loans off over ten years. Under this hypothetical scenario, the borrower decides to send in an extra $100 in order to pay off the loans more quickly.

It is at this point that the report explains that unless the borrower sent "explicit instructions on how to process her loan payment," the loan servicer is left with the task of deciding how to apply the extra $100 across her three loans.[59] While the borrower will indefinitely reduce long-term payments by paying off loans faster with the extra $100 payment, the amount of potential money saved can "vary widely depending on what the servicer chooses to do next."[60]

Moreover, while the borrower would save $219.47 if the additional payment was applied only to the loan with the highest interest rate, the servicer would also have the option of applying the payment evenly across all three loans, reducing the savings to just $149.82.[61]

This has the potential to accumulate to significant amounts over time, in that if the borrower continued to submit an additional $100 for every monthly payment, the savings deficit would continue to compound. For example, if the servicer decided to divide the extra $100 per month evenly between the three loans, it would add up to a savings of $4,514.98, compared to a savings of $5,403.62 if it was applied only to the loan with the highest interest rate.[62]

Consumer complaints suggest that "instead of applying extra payments to the loans with the highest interest rates," most online payment platforms are set up in a way that maximizes the payment period and the amount paid as a result.[63]

In addition to applying "underpayment" plans in order to "maximize late fees charged to borrowers,"[64] consumers also reported difficulties finding "accurate payoff information from servicers," who were told "different payoff amounts from different customer service representatives" that would often result in such underpayments and irrevocable late fees.[65]

Consistent with these industry-wide complaints were accusations made explicitly against Sallie Mae. In *United States ex rel. Batiste v.*

SLM Corp., a former employee of a Sallie Mae subsidiary claimed that Sallie Mae had "unlawfully placed loans into forbearance, allowing SLM to increase its return on the loans through accruing interest and also artificially maintain a low default ratio, which was required to maintain eligibility as a FFELP lender under Department of Education guidelines."[66]

Although the case was dismissed on a first-to-file provision of the FCA,[67] the substantive claims in this case are eerily similar to those made against firms in the for-profit higher education industry, which were guilty of placing loans in deferment or forbearance in order to stay below the 30 percent default ceiling as a means to remain eligible for federal aid.

While these offenses are troubling enough on their own, additional complaints of improper treatment of military borrowers sheds further light on the servicing flaws of the student lending industry.

According to an FDIC investigation, Sallie Mae was also in violation of the Servicemembers Civil Relief Act, "a federal law intended to alleviate certain legal, administrative, and financial pressures on active-duty members of the military."[68] Making "improper demands"[69] of active-duty servicemembers, further testimony reveals that many of the incentives driving for-profit abuses of "military education benefits" under Title IV of the Higher Education Act also exist with private lenders as well.[70]

In the end, veterans are only a small portion of students who have become victims of the very firm that was created to help them. By manipulating the student lending market in a way that poses minimal risk to lenders, colleges are able to raise tuition to compete by maximizing prestige and satisfy amenity demand from students without absorbing the associated costs. In turn, lenders are happy to oblige by servicing more loans, because higher tuition ultimately means larger returns on the interest.

As student lenders reap exorbitant profit margins from frivolous college spending on unnecessary luxury items and services, students are reduced to rags in bearing the brunt of the cost. We are a part of a system that is as rigged as it is unsustainable. If balance is not restored with reforms to the market soon, the collapse of the entire system and the unknown consequences that will result are inevitable.

The industry is in need of a profound realignment of priorities, above all in restoring long-term student success as the primary objective. From this will come a redefinition of the very purpose of higher education—one that shifts the focus from simple access and affordability to a higher goal of ensuring that investments from both students and taxpayers alike are not made in vain.

ESSENTIAL TAKEAWAYS

From a small secondary market supplier of funds to preserve liquidity and stability in the student loan market, Sallie Mae eventually sought a way to successfully privatize by the early 1990s. Following a series of negotiations, a deal allowing for privatization was settled upon in 1996, granting Sallie Mae a lengthy transition period and several market advantages by which the company was able to privatize and profit.

These negotiations were effectively made under false pretenses, however, as a significantly more aggressive board took control of the company following the negotiation period. Abusing many of the provisions intended to ensure a smooth transition period, Sallie Mae systematically bought most of its smaller regional competitors between 1999 and 2004, creating a highly complex and profitable corporate structure that infiltrated every component of the student lending industry.

During this same period, Sallie Mae also lobbied for several amendments to the Higher Education Act that virtually removed all avenues of discharge from student loans by 2005, rigging a market with minimal risk in their favor. Since then, Sallie Mae has reorganized itself again by splitting itself into two entities to separate old portfolios serviced under FFELP from the new private loan originations that will build the future of the company under the Sallie Mae Bank. This has allowed Sallie Mae to take control of a majority of the market share, reducing its competitors to a minimal threat.

Sallie Mae's market share dominance poses significant concerns to borrowers, as Sallie Mae has fielded a majority of complaints ranging from problems with debt-collection practices to making improper demands of active-duty military personnel seeking benefits under the Servicemembers Civil Relief Act. Ultimately, Sallie Mae strategically positioned itself to take control of the student lending market during its privatization period and has since taken further steps to capitalize on its market dominance for the future.

7

BREAKING BACKS TO BALANCE BUDGETS

Although private lenders have worked to encourage and facilitate the systematic flaws that are responsible for creating an unsustainable trend in the costs of college, they are not the only entity that profits from the status quo.

Prior to 2010, there were two primary methods of funding and supplying federal student loans. Under the original Federal Family Education Loan Program (FFELP), there existed a series of money transactions that began with funds that flowed into banks and other financial institutions from investors.[1]

From there, money was then distributed to guarantee agencies, which was then funneled to FFELP lenders that would service loans either owned by themselves or the Department of Education.[2] Remember, it was these "guaranteed loans" under FFELP that large private lenders, such as Sallie Mae, were able to service and collect record profits from the interest and transaction fees as a result.

Contrary to this complicated process of lucrative money transactions and fees that were assessed in the process, the Federal Direct Lending Program (FDLP) was originally created under the 1993 Budget Act to stand as a simplified alternative. These loans were "funded by low-cost borrowing from the U.S. Treasury" to the Department of Education, which would lend the money directly to students.[3] After operating as a two-pronged lending system for seventeen years, the structure of federal student lending underwent a fundamental transformation in 2010, following the passage of the Health Care and Education Reconciliation Act.

Initially proposed on July 15, 2009, as the Student Aid and Fiscal Responsibility Act (SAFRA) by George Miller, chairman of the House Committee on Education and Labor, Congress took the initiative to end FFELP for good. However, due to concerns over not having enough votes to override a filibuster[4] in the Senate, the legislation was eventually passed as a budget amendment under budget reconciliation, which only requires fifty-one votes for passage.[5]

Although there were several minor concessions made between SA-FRA and the Health Care and Education Reconciliation Act as a result of this conversion to a budget reconciliation measure, a majority of the substance under the former was ultimately passed with the latter. Arguably the most significant provision of the law calls for the "Termination of Federal Family Education Loan Appropriations" under part II—"Student Loan Reform"—by which "no funds are authorized to be appropriated . . . for which the first disbursement is after June 30, 2010."[6]

While old loans originated under FFELP prior to June 30, 2010, are still being serviced in mass amounts, such as Sallie Mae's $118.1 billion in related portfolios, this effectively eliminates the future of guaranteed loans under FFELP and replaces them with direct loans under the FDLP. Because Sallie Mae will eventually lose a massive amount of potential portfolios as a result of this provision, we begin to understand the recent decision by Sallie Mae to split into two entities, which has led to substantial growth in private loan portfolios.

Aside from eliminating an inefficient FFELP and its subsequent impact on Sallie Mae, there are several other positive features of this legislation. The first is an investment of $40 billion in Pell Grants, expanding the maximum grant award from $5,550 in 2013 to $5,975 in 2017.[7] This change is largely intended to keep pace with the rising costs of college and ensure that low-income families are adequately subsidized. Additionally, the law also secures $2.55 billion in mandatory funding for Historically Black Colleges and Universities and Minority-Serving Institutions, which enroll nearly 60 percent of the 4.7 million minority undergraduates in higher education today.[8]

While the legislation ensures greater assistance to low-income and minority households, the law offers several additional opportunities that are more widely available. One of these provisions includes an expansion of the Income-Based Repayment (IBR) program, which allows borrowers who assume loans after July 1, 2014, to cap their student loans at 10 percent of their discretionary income, on top of having the balance forgiven after twenty years, so long as payments are made during the twenty-year repayment period.[9]

In conjunction with broad assistance on repayment, the law also provides $2 billion over four years for community colleges, which house approximately 80 percent of all undergraduate enrollment.[10] According to the Obama Administration, these "resources will help community colleges and other institutions develop, improve, and provide education and career training programs suitable for workers who are eligible for trade adjustment assistance," which will be "housed at the Department of Labor and implemented in close cooperation with the Department of Education."[11]

While each of these provisions is helpful to lower- and middle-income families across the country, there are still several flaws with the federal student loan program. Before discussing the inherent problems of the present-day system, it is important to understand the specific mechanics and full scope of the program as it operates today.

There are currently several types of federal student loans that college students are potentially eligible for, all offering a wide range of rules and interest rates. Two of the most common loans are Direct Subsidized Loans and Direct Unsubsidized Loans, largely referred to as Stafford Loans.

Direct Subsidized Loans are available to undergraduate students with financial need, which is determined by a number of factors ranging from household income to material assets. For Direct Subsidized Loans, "the U.S. Department of Education pays the interest on a Direct Subsidized Loan while you're in school at least half-time, for the first six months after you leave school (referred to as a grace period), and during a period of deferment (a postponement of loan payments)."[12]

On the other hand, Direct Unsubsidized Loans hold "no requirement to demonstrate financial need," and the school you have chosen to attend "determines the amount you can borrow based on your cost of attendance and other financial aid you receive."[13] Unlike Direct Subsidized Loans, students "are responsible for paying the interest on a Direct Unsubsidized Loan during all periods" and "if you choose not to pay the interest while you are in school, during grace periods and deferment[14] or forbearance[15] periods, your interest will accrue (accumulate) and be capitalized (that is, your interest will be added to the principal amount of your loan)."[16]

Despite the differences in interest payment requirements, the interest rate itself for both of these loans disbursed between July 1, 2013, and June 30, 2014, amounted to 3.86 percent.[17] However, Direct Unsubsidized Loans carry with them a 5.41 percent interest rate for loans disbursed during this same period to graduate and professional students.[18]

An additional feature of these loans also includes an annual increase on the loan limits students are eligible for on a year-to-year basis. First-year dependent undergraduate students are eligible for a total of $5,500 in Stafford Loans, where no more than $3,500 may amount to subsidized loans.[19] This increases to a total of $6,500 for second-year undergraduate students, where no more than $4,500 may be subsidized loans.[20] Furthermore, dependent students in the third or fourth year of their undergraduate studies are eligible for $7,500 in Stafford Loans, where no more than $5,500 may be in subsidized.[21] This translates to an aggregate loan limit for Stafford Loans that amounts to $31,000, of which no more than $23,000 is allowed to be subsidized.

Aside from these baseline subsidized and unsubsidized loans under the FDLP, Direct PLUS Loans have become increasingly utilized by households that are sending students to college. There are two types of borrowers who are eligible for a Direct PLUS Loan. These include graduate students "enrolled at least half-time at an eligible school in a program leading to a degree or certificate," as well as "parents (biological, adoptive, or in some cases, step-parent) of a dependent undergraduate student enrolled at least half-time at a participating school."[22]

Not only do both graduate students and parents of dependent undergraduate students share the option of placing loans into deferment while the student is "enrolled at least half-time and for an additional six months after the students ceases to be enrolled at least half-time," but they also pay a 6.41 percent interest rate on loans disbursed between July 1, 2013, and June 30, 2014.[23]

In addition to Direct Subsidized and Unsubsidized Loans under the Stafford Program, as well as the Direct PLUS Loans that are largely taken on by graduate students and parents of dependent undergraduate students, Federal Perkins Loans are particularly important as a major

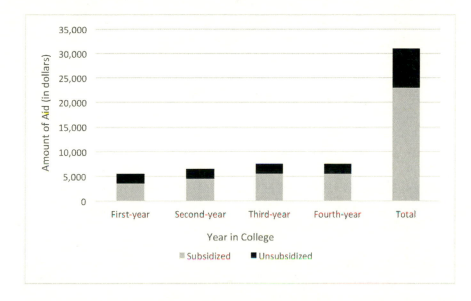

Figure 7.1.   Annual Fluctuations in Stafford Loan Eligibility.   *Source: "Federal Student Aid, Direct Subsidized and Unsubsidized Loans," U.S. Department of Education, 2014, http://studentaid.ed.gov/types/loans/subsidized-unsubsidized#what%27s-the-difference (accessed February 8, 2014).*

source of funding "for undergraduate and graduate students with exceptional financial need."[24]

While undergraduate students "may be eligible to receive up to $5,500 a year," capped at a total amount of $27,500, graduate students "may be eligible to receive up to $8,000 per year," amounting to a total of $60,000 after including amounts borrowed as an undergraduate.[25] Additionally, Federal Perkins Loans disbursed between July 1, 2013, and June 30, 2014, carry with them a 5 percent interest rate, upon which repayment begins "nine months after you graduate, leave school, or drop below half-time status."[26]

Although there is already plenty of confusion in regard to different eligibility requirements, interest rates, and loan limits, further complication surrounds the various repayment options that students have to choose from.

The first of these options is this Standard Repayment Plan. Applicable to Direct Subsidized and Unsubsidized Loans, as well as all Direct PLUS Loans, payments are set at a fixed amount of at least $50 per month for up to ten years, ultimately leading the borrower to pay less interest for the loan over time, relative to many of the other plans.[27]

Another repayment option is the Graduated Repayment Plan. Applicable to the same loan types under the Standard Repayment Plan, this option allows for payments to be lower at first, with gradual increases every two years for a ten-year period.[28] While this accommodates borrowers with low starting salaries upon entering the workforce, the total amount paid on the loan will be more than the amount paid under the Standard Repayment Plan as a result of paying off interest less quickly.

Aside from these two ten-year plans for Direct Loans, there are several additional repayment options. The Extended Repayment Plan, relevant to the same loan types as its ten-year counterparts with a minimum of $30,000 in outstanding loan debt, allows for either fixed or graduated payments for up to twenty-five years.[29] This means that while the monthly payments are significantly lower than ten-year plans, the borrower will ultimately pay much more over time under the extended repayment option.

In addition to this first type of extended repayment option, there are several other options for borrowers who can prove partial financial hardship, one being the Income-Based Repayment Plan. Under an IBR Plan, each of the loan types included in the previous plans are covered in addition to consolidated loans,[30] under which monthly payments account for 15 percent of the borrower's discretionary income,[31] and adjusts as discretionary income fluctuates for up to twenty-five years.[32]

While monthly payments will be lower than those under the ten-year standard plan, borrowers will still pay more for the loan over time relative to the ten-year alternative. However, there is a special provision under this plan that forgives an outstanding balance on the loan after making the equivalent of twenty-five years in qualifying monthly payments, which is a large factor in attracting borrowers to choose the IBR option.[33]

Much like an IBR Plan, a "Pay as You Earn" Repayment Plan is also an option for borrowers. Relevant to Direct Subsidized and Unsubsidized Loans, as well as Direct PLUS Loans made only to independent graduate students (excluding the parents of dependent undergraduate students), maximum monthly payments are 10 percent of the borrower's discretionary income, and fluctuates in the same manner as payments under IBR Plans.[34] Additionally, the same loan forgiveness mechanism is also built into this repayment option; however, the payment period is twenty years, unlike the twenty-five-year timetable under IBR Plans.[35]

There is also an Income-Contingent Repayment Plan, which can be applied to the identical loan types and conditions set under the "Pay as You Earn" Repayment Plans, with the addition of Direct Consolidation Loans. Under this option, payments are calculated each year and are based on the borrower's adjusted gross income, family size, and the total amount of Direct Loans owed.[36] Consistent with comparable repayment plans, the payments change as the borrower's income changes, and the same balance forgiveness applies after the equivalent of twenty-five years in qualifying monthly payments has been reached.[37]

Lastly, there is the Income-Sensitive Repayment Plan, which applies to the remaining FFELP Stafford Loans, FFELP PLUS Loans, and FFELP Consolidation Loans that are no longer originated but continue to be repaid under portfolios originated prior to June 30, 2010. For these remaining loans, monthly payments are based on annual income, and borrowers with FFELP loans that are not owned by the Department of Education are subject to varying formulas between different lending firms.[38]

Although this range of eligibility requirements, interest rates, loan limits, and repayment options for federal student loans is complicated enough, recent legislation has worked to compound the confusion that had already existed prior to its enactment. As a consequence of the timetable set on federal student loans under the College Cost Reduction and Access Act of 2007, interest rate reductions of Federal Stafford Loans were set to expire on July 1, 2013, causing them to double from 3.4 percent back to the original rate of 6.8 percent.[39]

Amid contentious debate in Congress over the summer of 2013, the final bill that was ultimately signed into law was the Bipartisan Student Loan Certainty Act of 2013. Spearheaded by House Republicans and supported by the Obama Administration, this law effectively ends the past policy of Congress determining a fixed interest rate under the College Cost Reduction and Access Act, and replaces it with the original system of attaching interest rates to ten-year Treasury bonds.[40]

Ten-year Treasury bonds are "one of the many government securities that are available to investors. The yield on the ten-year Treasury note, which fluctuates based on supply and demand, is often used as an economic indicator."[41] Because interest rates are determined by the market value of Treasury bonds that are currently valued at marginally low rates, Congress has temporarily prevented federal student loan interest rates from doubling. As a result, each of the federal loan types issued between June 30, 2013, and June 30, 2014, hold the following annual fixed rates: Direct Subsidized Loans at 3.86 percent, Direct Unsubsidized Loans at 5.41 percent, and Direct PLUS Loans at 6.41 percent.[42]

In order to gain enough support from Senate Democrats, the law also provides interest rate caps for each of these loans as a way to safeguard against interest rates from becoming exorbitantly high if the value of ten-year Treasury bonds spike. These include interest rate caps of 8.25 percent for Direct Subsidized Loans, 9.5 percent for Direct Unsubsidized Loans, and 10.5 percent for Direct PLUS Loans.[43]

Although the current interest rates, set by the market value of ten-year Treasury bonds, are significantly lower than these caps, recent reports suggest that this will fail to be the case in just a few short years. These future projections estimate that by 2018, interest rates on Direct Subsidized Loans will be 7.25 percent, while Direct Unsubsidized Loans will be marked at 8.88 percent, and Direct PLUS Loans at 9.8 percent.[44]

As Senator Elizabeth Warren suggests, the Bipartisan Student Loan Certainty Act initially offers a "teaser-rate student loan system."[45] Supporting his colleague's remarks, Senator Jack Reed has also expressed concern over attaching interest rates to ten-year Treasury bonds, claiming that it will "add more to students' debt than if the Senate did nothing," and allowed the interest rates to simply double to 6.8 percent.[46] Whether or not the interest rates on federal student loans will actually reach the caps, a recent report suggests that federal student loans will still largely remain cheaper than private loan alternatives, which can reach interest rates of up to 18 percent.[47]

While it is true that the interest rates on federal student loans are significantly lower than their private counterparts, there have been recent objections by several members of Congress as to how generous the federal government actually is in regard to the interest rates that have been set. According to recent data collected by the Congressional Budget Office, the federal government made $51 billion in profits from the interest on federal student loans in 2013 alone.[48]

Emphasizing this point, Senator Warren has emerged as a leading critic of the federal student loan program as it exists today. Given the incredible financial stress placed on households that are sending family members to college, Senator Warren proposed her first solution to alleviate such pressure with the Bank on Students Loan Fairness Act on May 8, 2013. In her opening remarks on the bill's proposal, Senator Warren explained that while "a big bank can get a loan through the Federal Reserve discount window at a rate of about 0.75 percent . . . a student who is trying to get a loan to go to college will pay almost 7 percent."[49]

Working from the basic premise that "we shouldn't be profiting from our students who are drowning in debt, while giving a great deal to the banks," Senator Warren went ahead to propose the Bank on Students Loan Fairness Act.[50] It provides that Federal Direct Stafford Loans shall "be available at interest rates that are equivalent to the interest rates at which the Federal Government provides loans to banks through the discount widow operated by the Federal Reserve System," and that "the applicable rate of interest shall be the primary credit rate charged by the Federal Reserve banks" under the Federal Reserve Act.[51] This would essentially apply a 0.75 percent interest rate to Federal Direct Stafford Loans.

Although the Bank on Students Loan Fairness Act was eventually overlooked in the Senate for the Bipartisan Student Loan Certainty Act,[52] Senator Warren's proposal is a far more cohesive remedy for a federal student loan market that is riddled with confusion and potentially high interest rates. However, before looking forward to possible solutions for the future of federal student lending, it is important to revisit the purpose of such a program in the first place.

It is important to remember the justification for providing federal tax revenue to subsidize and ultimately create our modern system of American higher education is rooted in the National Defense of Education Act of 1958.[53]

> The security of the Nation requires the fullest development of the mental resources and technical skills of its young men and women. The present emergency demands that additional and more adequate educational opportunities be made available. The defense of this Nation depends upon the mastery of modern techniques developed from complex scientific principles. It depends as well upon the dis-

covery and development of new principles, new techniques, and new knowledge. [54]

Lawmakers understood that a modern system of higher education was vital in the mission of preserving America's status as a preeminent world power in the future. Applying federal tax revenue in an investment to train the future innovators of America's workforce, the NDEA, which stands as the foundation for every subsequent higher education policy, essentially ensured the well-being of the nation by protecting the financial security of its students.

Since 1958, however, it is apparent that Congress has deviated from this simple and practical mission. Compared to offering minimal interest rates and simple repayment plans, recent decisions by Congress have led college students, the supposed investment, down a path of high interest rates, red tape on loan options, and complicated repayment plans.

Our federal investment in higher education has fundamentally transformed from one that seeks to put students through school so that they might better affect the economy, to one focused on making an immediate profit off of the interest. Given this understanding, there is a clear course of action that can be taken to restore our federal investment in higher education in a way that benefits the student and the general economy, rather than Congress seeking to close deficits on the backs of its supposed investment.

The first remedy is to simply extend Senator Warren's proposal of a fixed 0.75 percent interest rate on Direct Stafford Loans to *all* loans made under the FDLP. Some critics of Senator Warren's proposal, such as Jonathan Z. Zhou of the *Harvard Crimson*, highlight that this interest rate is "only available to banks in good financial condition and provide collateral for their loans," and should not be available to the "risky long-term loans made to individuals without credit history and collateral." [55] From the assessment of low-risk versus high-risk borrowers, Zhou goes on to suggest that it would not be wise to apply a 0.75 percent interest rate on federal student loans as a result.

However, there is a key component to the federal student lending system that Zhou, and those who agree with him, have missed. In a 1978 amendment to the U.S. Bankruptcy Code, any "program funded in whole or in part by a governmental unit or nonprofit institution" is exempt from discharge.[56] This was essentially installed to protect federal taxpayers against tax revenue being discharged under bankruptcy, effectively removing the "risk" that Zhou highlights.

Furthermore, if the federal student lending industry did base interest rates on risk, as is commonly practiced in the private industry, why would Direct PLUS Loans, largely borrowed by parents with established careers, credit, and collateral, carry with them higher interest rates than Direct Stafford Loans that are borrowed by students with little to no established career, credit, or collateral? The simple fact is that the protections under U.S. Bankruptcy Code are enough to shield taxpayers from this risk, therefore rendering such concerns null and void.

With the question of risk and its role in determining federal student loan interest rates resolved, there seems to be no reason that explains why a 0.75 percent interest rate should not apply to all federal student loans. This not only will undo the system of interest rates attached to ten-year Treasury notes under the Bipartisan Student Loan Certainty Act, but will also remove the profit made by Congress off of the interest. Consequently, students will be alleviated from much of the financial burden associated with federal student loans, restoring the program to a truly "subsidized" system.

In addition to eliminating the profit made off of federal student loans by reducing interest rates to 0.75 percent, it is also important to simplify the highly complicated system of repayment options that exist today. With the various interest rates that are tied to ten-year Treasury notes eliminated, there should be no need for a series of complicated repayment plans that are meant to tackle the variety of interest rates that currently exist.

From the many repayment options that exist today, the most practical and comprehensive type of repayment seems to be the Income-Based Repayment Plan. Just to refresh our memories, each of the loan types that are covered by the Standard Repayment Plan are included with the addition of consolidated loans, by which monthly payments account for 15 percent of the borrower's discretionary income, and adjusts as discretionary income changes for up to twenty-five years.

This plan is particularly effective, in that it guards against harming those who are unable to find a high-paying job by the time repayments are issued, in that it will be 15 percent of the borrower's discretionary income, no matter how low that income might be. In other words, it avoids many of the problems associated with repayment under Standard Repayment, which demands a fixed monthly payment regardless of the borrower's income.[57]

Additionally, the special provision under this plan that forgives an outstanding balance on the loan after making the equivalent of twenty-five years in qualifying monthly payments also seems to be a practical component built into this plan. While an overwhelming majority of borrowers will not need to take advantage of this added protection, it will ensure that college graduates with the least financial security are safeguarded as they approach retirement.

Although these advancements surrounding federal student loans are a step in the right direction, the majority of the problem remains unsolved. While the interest of a loan surely adds up over time, it is ultimately the principal amount of the payment that defines the severity of its financial burden to the borrower. While federal student interest rates are surely a part of the equation, it is ultimately the escalating price of college that directly influences the amount of the principal.

For a solution, the attention of this discussion must therefore be refocused from restoring the mission of the federal student lending program to redefining the priorities of the colleges themselves. We have clearly outlined factors driving the behaviors of colleges in chapters 2 and 3, as well as the actions taken on behalf of the lending industry to enable and perpetuate such behaviors in chapters 4–7. The purpose of the next chapter will be to offer bold solutions that are successful in restructuring a higher education market with a primary focus of benefiting the student, not the market at the student's expense.

ESSENTIAL TAKEAWAYS

Federal student lending began with a very simple structure and premise—help students afford to go to college. Over the years, this mission has been compromised by a confusing variety of loans, interest rates, and repayment options. Moreover, Congress has manipulated the system from one that is intended to serve the needs of students to one where the federal government profits from tens of billions of dollars in interest.

Equally as egregious as the federal government making attempts to balance the budget off of the backs of students—people with the least financial security in this country—is the recent arrangement that transform fixed interest rates to flexible interest rates attached to ten-year Treasury notes. This lending scheme was passed with misrepresentation, advertising artificially low interest rates with the knowledge that they would increase as inflation grew over time.

There is a simple proposal—adopt and expand the proposal already drafted by Senator Elizabeth Warren. Detach interest rates from ten-year Treasury notes and lower them to be fixed at 0.75 percent. This would eliminate the practice of the government profiting off of college students. This rate, however, should extend to all loans, because it is equally unfair to balance budgets on the backs of graduate students and parents trying to help their children pay for college as well. With interest rates settled, proposals should further simplify the repayment model, reducing repayment to a single IBR Plan that would protect any student or parent from having their entire paycheck stripped and funneled to repaying their college debt burden. This proposal returns federal lending to a policy of service committed to protecting students and parents, not profiting from them.

8

A STAKE IN THE GAME

In recent years, college enrollment has grown to unprecedented levels, not seen during any other period in our nation's history. This has largely been the result of an unspoken assurance that a college degree will lead to employment in an ever-more-competitive professional job market. This understanding, however, is not reflective of the reality that college graduates face upon turning from the classroom to the workforce. Simply put, the harsh reality is that just because a college offers a degree in a field of study, it does not necessarily mean that there is demand for employment in that given field.

Based upon recent unemployment reports, there seems to be a broad scope of degrees that do not have a positive return on investment for graduates. While it is true that college graduates have lower unemployment rates relative to people who only have a high school diploma, it is also clear that "not all degrees are created equal."[1]

Among recent graduates, many of the majors with the highest unemployment rates come from fields within the humanities, such as anthropology at 12.6 percent; film, video, and photographic arts at 11.4 percent; and English literature at 9.8 percent.[2] Additionally, similar unemployment rates can be found in the social sciences, such as sociology at 9.9 percent.[3]

Compounding the problem of unemployment in many of these fields, characterized as liberal arts degrees, the same figures apply to generic and mainstream majors such as business. Based on 40 million job profiles, a recent report suggests that those who majored in business administration and management are 8.2 times more likely to be under-employed than their peers with more specialized degrees in a particular field of the business industry, such as finance.[4]

Although it has been argued that higher education serves many purposes across different institutional tiers, there is one objective that is shared at all levels of the college system. This common purpose is generally understood as a pathway to employment in a career related to the field of an individual's study and degree. While this is certainly not the only function of a college education, it is arguably the most fundamental and essential component that drives students to pursue a degree in higher learning.

Given this baseline premise, the inevitable question that follows concerns the statistics provided above. Why, if one of the assumed primary purposes of higher education is to provide a pathway to employment within the relevant field of study, are there so many people finding themselves unemployed and underemployed upon graduation? The unfortunate answer is that because of incentives that colleges follow in the quest for maximizing prestige, what is assumed by students to be a priority of colleges is actually not a priority at all.

Considering how an expansion of programs can be used as a way to increase an institution's rank, in addition to attracting a larger pool of applicants as a result of satisfying a broader student demand, why would any college choose to cut programs that are not leading graduates to employment, so long as students continue to be assured that any degree will lead to employment reflective of that degree? In other words, the flaws of the current arrangement inevitably lead colleges to compete in a way that favors providing *false* opportunity over *real* opportunity.

As a consequence of the combined incentives with inaccurate student perception, the supposed watchers of the flock more resemble wolves than shepherds. Exploiting the widely held misconceptions of students, it is the students who ultimately fall victim to the very institutions they place their trust in. As a result, the key to reversing this trend is to curb the priorities of colleges in a way that is reflective of the students they serve.

A plan that will effectively change how colleges behave requires a two-fold solution. The first of these is to simply apply information that already exists in a way that incentivizes colleges to value quality over quantity. Under President Obama's proposal for a "college scorecard," the Department of Education collects data on "undergraduate enrollment, costs, graduation rate, loan default rate, median borrowing, and employment."[5]

Under the Higher Education Opportunity Act of 2008 (HEOA), institutions that receive Title IV assistance from federal student financial aid programs must submit this information on an annual basis if they are to remain eligible for such funds.[6] This is particularly useful when determining information, current and projected, regarding one's ability to place a monetary value on their degree in terms of job placement and earnings potential.

Today, the only way in which this information may be applied is by making it available for students to view on the Department of Education webpage via the college calculator.[7] There, students currently have access to all of this information, ranging from "loan default rate" to "job placement," and are then charged with the task of weighing their options and deciding which institution to attend.

While this appears to be a fairly innovative plan at the surface, there are several inherent flaws within this technique. The first can be found in the assumption that prospective students will visit the site and reflect thoughtfully upon the information provided. If we have learned anything from this discussion, it is that the college application process is in many ways overwhelming. Prospective students are bombarded with information upon applying for college in everything from student loans to off-campus housing; the list is endless.

Additionally, the current model assumes that all prospective students have a wide range of options when choosing a college. However, many prospective students have the possibility of being limited in the range of options they have for a series of reasons ranging from their academic merits to their financial capacity to pay for college. Case in point, Harvard has a very high "score" in the college scorecard system. Unfortunately, most students do not have a serious chance of being accepted into Harvard.

Although this is an extreme case, it demonstrates the fact that low-performing applicants who come from low-income families are incredibly limited in which options they have to choose from in reality. Consequently, as the status quo demonstrates, students are largely unaffected by the information currently at their disposal.

The second flaw concerns the fact that higher education is funded by large amounts of federal subsidies that are derived from taxpayer dollars. To be specific, the Department of Education distributed a total of $134 billion in student aid in 2014 alone.[8]

We have already established the premise that taxpayer money was first mobilized to invest broadly in higher education for the purpose of strengthening the economy, improving invocation, and ensuring national security. With this understanding, why would the federal government continue to subsidize colleges that undermine this central mission by making poor investments that do not maximize post-graduation performance? Currently, colleges and students alike virtually have free reign to make whatever decisions they wish in a system that is funded with hundreds of billions of dollars in taxpayer money. This is a serious problem, and one that can and should be fixed immediately.

The solution is simple: Attach institutional eligibility to Title IV financial aid funds to post-graduation performance. Although President Obama has hinted at adopting this model, I believe that there is a particular set of criteria that should be embraced in a very particular way, which deviates from the president's proposal in a few minor ways. Of the factors included in the current college scorecard, we would include "loan default rate" and "employment," while omitting "undergraduate enrollment," "costs," and "median borrowing." In addition to "loan default rate," and "employment," I would also add the "median salary" of graduates five years post-graduation.

This particular set of factors that I propose to be included in the model are those that are most reflective of the core challenge facing people in the college affordability crisis. My perception is that the cost of college itself actually is not the central concern; it is the ability to pay for the cost. Whether we like to recognize it or not, the job market places value on a degree not only in the frequency of its employment, but also in the size of the occupation's compensation as well.

If a college delivers degrees to students that are highly valued by the market in both of these categories, students are likely to have the financial capacity to pay off their student debt burden despite the cost. The basic thought here is that students should pay for what they get. Factors such as the "loan default rate," "employment rate," and "median salary" are the three most reliable indicators of the return on the student and taxpayer investment in any given student's education and long-term well-being.

As for the several factors we should omit from the calculations, there are three general reasons why each of the remaining features are not reliable. In terms of "undergraduate enrollment," encouraging higher enrollment not only fails to diminish the quantity-versus-quality problem of the status quo, but it also exacerbates it. By incentivizing colleges to continue enrolling more and more students, blind to what the job market demands, this factor would essentially undermine the mission of tailoring a college system that is reflective of job market demand altogether.

"Graduation rate" should also be avoided due to its potential to be skewed for a favorable outcome by colleges, in that institutions could simply reduce the level of rigor in order to promote higher rates of student *success*.

As for "costs" and "median borrowing," these factors have the possibility of inflicting several unintended and unnecessary consequences. In terms of borrowing rates, this could lead schools with small endowments, unable to provide large independent scholarships to low-income applicants, to reject applications from prospective students with little financial security. This could present the likely possibility of having an adverse effect on low-income students who, although academically capable, might be discriminated against in a form of risk-aversion by colleges.

Additionally, the "costs" section in general should not be a factor, because it does not accurately reflect the market value of the degree. So long as the graduate has obtained a degree that is highly valued by the market and the student is able to pay off those costs with a salary that is reflective of that high value, why should a college not be able to charge high tuition if the value is there?

After establishing the "loan default rate," "employment rate," and "median salary" as the three factors by which colleges are to be graded, the way in which these measurements are to be used stands as the next step. Applying these standards as a gauge for institutional value, colleges should be assessed a credit rating, based upon their "scorecard" of factors, which would then determine the amount of Title IV eligibility an institution qualifies for. For example, institutions with the highest levels of "value," based upon the three factors, would receive a "AAA" credit rating, and would therefore receive the maximum amount of federal aid allotted.

The rating system would then follow a regressive rewards system of federal aid, in that as the institution's credit rating diminishes, so does the amount of its federal aid. This would extend even to the point of colleges with the lowest ratings relinquishing all aid eligibility. Before this is a viable plan, however, a reform to the private student lending market must be made simultaneously. As mentioned earlier, the private lending market has been able to grow at a rapid pace as a result of reduced risk following an amendment to the Higher Education Act in 2005 that extends limits on student loan dischargability to private loans.[9]

With much of the risk alleviated from the private student lending industry, what stops a college from simply supplementing any lost aid with private student loans under the new credit rating system? Without rolling back this amendment, students would actually be progressively worse off, due to the correlation of lower-"value" degrees being supplemented more and more by higher-interest private loans as the "value" decreases. This means that the lowest-"value" degree recipients would also likely incur some of the highest long-term debt burdens as a result of holding more private loans with higher interest rates.

To avoid this, Congress would simply need to pass an additional amendment to the Higher Education Act that reinstates discharge capabilities through bankruptcy on private student loans, therefore injecting the appropriate risk back into the private student lending market and eliminating the widespread threat of private loans supplementing lost federal aid.

With colleges firmly dependent upon Title IV aid that is conditioned on student post-graduation performance, I anticipate institutions fundamentally realigning their priorities so that they are in harmony with the long-term interests of students and taxpayers—the consumers. Aside from a few extreme cases, colleges by and large receive federal aid despite how their graduates perform in the job market. With this new grading system, the primary focus of colleges will be to make sure that their graduates are equipped with degrees and skill sets that will make them competitive in the labor force. It turns a system that grades on what goes into the product into one that would rank institutions based upon student performance in the long run.

Faced with the consequence of losing Title IV student aid if their graduates fail to perform well in the job market, colleges will be inclined to cut programs that are leading graduates to unemployment and underemployment, while expanding upon or even creating new programs that will foster student success long after they have graduated. In order to assist colleges to meet these demands, I propose that the Bureau of Labor Statistics, which has data on ten-year employment projections by sector, should partner with the Department of Education to ensure that every college is aware of projected employment trends with enough time to adapt.[10]

To clarify, there are just a few key components to this model. The first comes with the federal government applying a standard that colleges must meet in order to remain eligible for different tiers of Title IV student aid. Colleges are then faced with several decisions, the first of which being to accept or refuse compliance with the new standard. With most colleges likely to comply out of necessity, institutions then have the freedom to choose which programs they need to cut, keep the same, expand, or create in order to satisfy the new standard.

From this, I expect most colleges to specialize in a limited number of studies. This resembles a higher education model proposed by William Patrick Leonard, known as the "Lean College." Most colleges will evolve into "ultra-low operating costs institutions" that "will be guided by a narrowly-focused mission statement."[11] Under the philosophy that "consumers need a no-frills university,"[12] colleges will be incentivized to "abandon the generic view-book pap that pervades the traditional higher education sectors. Rather, it will work with employers and graduate/professional schools in isolating the core knowledge and soft skills" that are necessary to compete in the job market.[13]

Although some might accuse this proposal of converting a majority of higher education institutions into glorified vocational schools, I am not particularly concerned about what we call our reformed system. Critics, in fact, would be justified in deeming this new system largely as a vocational model. However, I would argue that this should carry with it a positive and proud title, and not that of a negative connotation, for all this suggests is that we should not be wasteful with our time, money, and resources. Subscribing to the central mind-set that higher education serves the primary purpose of providing financial security to the individual as well as strength and innovation to the economy as a whole, this model is actually quite efficient in achieving that end.

There is the additional question of what happens to the traditional liberal arts model of providing more than occupational skills. Associated with this particular model are the fields that are considered to be "academic" in nature and intended to emphasize the process of "higher learning" to students, among other things. At first glance, such a model cannot possibly exist within the "Lean College" system.

Despite any initial misconceptions, this type of higher education will be preserved indefinitely. In a perfect world, it would be ideal to offer a universal liberal arts education to everyone. However, as the status quo demonstrates, this model is as infeasible and unsustainable, as it is impractical and unproductive to the taxpayer return on investment. Certain degrees, across all fields, have proven to be ineffective for positive student outcomes following graduation. There is no agenda to promote one specific program over the next, but only to eliminate the parasitic drain of degrees that hurl graduates into a lifetime of financial ruin.

Just as the job market fails to demand that everyone obtain a degree in medicine, so is the case with traditional liberal arts degrees. With that said, as there is the demand for x number of doctors, so is the case for positions in the liberal arts. The task, as is the case with every other field, is to ensure that there is a proper balance in the supply relative to market demand.

Because such demand is largely concentrated and constrained to academia, the supply necessary to meet demand is relatively small. Therefore, I suspect that liberal arts studies will become limited to the top-performing institutions in the country as a result of colleges naturally cutting programs, including liberal arts, which are predominantly leading graduates to underemployment and unemployment under the status quo. Although such a threshold is not predefined by any stretch of the imagination, and colleges will have the freedom to pick and choose which programs they decide to keep and eliminate, the overall trend will be that of a college market that is responsive to job market demand in every sector.

With the top universities having the capacity to solely satisfy market demand, colleges in the middle and lower tiers of the entire higher education system will likely cut many of its liberal arts programs because market demand will have already been fulfilled. Consequently, there is the critique that this system will limit opportunity to many average- and low-performing students from studying fields they are most interested in because the caliber of college they are admitted into will have cut that particular program to comply with federal aid eligibility requirements.

In response, we should be promoting and investing in a higher education system that provides *real* long-term opportunity in the form of employment prospects and increased earnings potential. Promoting any field that leads a majority of its students into unemployment or underemployment is simply not *real* opportunity. Plainly stated, the illusion of job security is not *real* opportunity; it is *false* opportunity. Returning to the fact that higher education is largely funded with hundreds of billions of dollars in federal subsidies each year, how can we possibly justify such a significant public investment in *false* opportunity? The simple answer is that we can no longer afford to make these poor investments.

Until recently, the only model for college financial planning was to independently hire a financial consultant, which cost a family trying to send their child to college from roughly $3,000 to upwards of $10,000 depending upon the geographic location. This type of assistance is expensive and ultimately unaffordable for most Americans. In Rochester, New York, however, three innovative entrepreneurs have set out to pioneer an affordable, interactive, and comprehensive financial consulting system for college students and their parents with the launch of College Assistance Plan through CAP Advisory Services, Inc. (CAP) in 2015.[14]

The founders of CAP, Richard Bannister, Steve Day, and Phil James, have found a new way for families to access these services through their employers' benefit programs. When we think of employee benefits, people traditionally relate to services like healthcare, disability, and life insurance benefits provided by employers. However, in a job market of growing competition, employers are beginning to offer employees "lifestyle benefits," which are primarily centered around financial wellness.

The incentive for employers is that when their employees are stable and financially sound, they are more productive and add greater value to the business. While most established lifestyle benefits programs of-

fered by employers center around retirement and other general financial areas, they do not deal with the enormous financial impact of college. The founders of CAP realize that college debt often touches all
areas of financial wellness. College is not only financed by student loans
but also funds redirected from home equity and 401k accounts. This
can have a devastating effect on overall financial goals for the average
family.

CAP was launched in 2015 as a product within the empolyee benefits market. Employers can provide this package for a very small price as
part of their overall employee benefits portfolio. As a result, employees
then have unlimited access to a robust site that aggregates everything
necessary to easily navigate the college process including a College
Roadmap and tools to help parents negotiate with colleges for lower
tuitions. The site also includes an interactive cost comparison tool between institutions and repayment trajectories that help families make
the best decisions possible. No longer do you have to spend hours
looking for the tools to be successful; CAP has it all.

Ultimately, CAP has exclusively pioneered a way to make college
financial planning widely available to for all American families. As Richard Bannister of CAP has said, "Our mission is to serve the average
American family who desperately needs help navigating this complex
process. Our program gives families the tools they need to lower their
cost, save time and ultimately make better long term decisions." This
point is crucial. In a world where every stage of higher education continues to become more unaffordable to Main Street America, CAP has
established an immediate solution. Included as an employee benefit,
employees are able to access these resources for free, as provided by
the employer. At no cost to the household, families are able to access
this resource and move toward minimizing their college debt burdens
as they continue to wait for the sweeping regulations that are necessary
to cure the college affordability crisis.

ESSENTIAL TAKEAWAYS

Today, it is only the students who have a stake in their fate. Even if a
student fails once they leave college, the colleges continue to rise in the
ranks and erect flashy new buildings. The lenders continue to squeeze

every drop they can from the debtors, and Congress continues to sit idly by, raking in tens of billions of dollars in profit from the federal loan interest. Modern history tells us that this system is no longer sustainable—it never was.

To provoke the changes necessary to avoid the ticking time bomb of the student debt bubble, the system must spread the stake in the game to everyone, not just the students. With a new mutual incentive to ensure long-term student success, colleges and lenders will react accordingly. The era of *every* college offering *every* degree to *everyone* who applies needs to end. Bold action, inspired by practicality, is the only chance we have in prevailing over the gluttonous and unsustainable system that threatens to destroy us if we do nothing.

9

THE *NEW* AMERICAN COLLEGE AND UNIVERSITY

We have learned what higher education has been in the past, and we know what it has become today. More important than understanding what *was* and *is*, we must determine a vision for what higher education *ought to be* for future generations. For if we do not choose carefully, it could all come crashing down upon us in our oblivion.

As an idea, what is higher education—a place for soul searching or job training, home for the few or the many, subjects dominated by the humanities or the sciences? Perhaps searching for a single answer to that question is misguided to begin with. In the United States, over 7,200 postsecondary institutions of higher education stand today.[1] There cannot possibly be a single answer that appropriately fits each and every one of these institutions.

Yet, we know from today's model of making available more and more to compete, institutions have developed a model that offers everything and anything to students in virtually the same fashion. Speaking over 150 years ago, Francis Wayland at Brown University warned against colleges "becoming more and more superficial," offering many subjects "in diluted quantities" with the consequence of creating graduates "who were not expert in anything."[2]

While some, including myself, fear that Wayland's nightmare has become a reality, others would disagree. Responding to criticisms made in 1827 against Yale for failing to change its curriculum for modern purposes, its professors "argued that such men needed a classical course far more than they needed a practical course."[3] As one professor said,

> Is it not desirable that the new men of wealth and influence being created by American abundance should be men of superior education, of a large and liberal views, of those solid and elegant attainments, which will raise them to a higher distinction, than the mere possession of property; which will not allow them to hoard their treasures, or waste them in senseless extravagance; which will enable them to adorn society by their learning, to move in the more intelligent circles with dignity and to make such an application of their wealth, as will be most honorable to themselves, and most beneficial to their country?[4]

This logic rests largely upon the assumption that any degree from any institution of higher education automatically translates to wealth and influence—a misconception held by many in America today. We must come to terms that this simply is not the case and that a "superior education" and "elegant attainments" do nothing to benefit students or their country if they do not generate adequate wealth and influence with that education.

What is meant by *wealth* and *influence*, and do we measure these terms in relation to the individual or society? We cannot be sure what the professors at Yale intended to mean by wealth and influence in 1827, but I define the *wealth* and *influence* of a college education in the twenty-first century in broad and humble terms.

For *wealth*, did the college education create a positive return on investment? In other words, I am not claiming that higher education must make people rich for it to be considered a success. Rather, did the college degree elevate the student to a career that allows for them to be self-sustaining over the course of their lifetime?

Do graduates earn enough of a living that allows them to pay their bills, purchase groceries, buy a home or start a family if they wish to, save for retirement, and invest in the things that bring joy to their lives—go to a concert, visit a museum, attend a professional sporting event, travel the world? These are not measures of the super wealthy, and I do not claim that the purpose of a higher education is to make people rich and rich alone.

In other words, did a college education help a person achieve a decent standard of life—the American Dream? For if higher education is to exist as Frederick Rudolph's "American College & University," what greater purpose can there be than to elevate its students to the middle class so that they may share in the American Dream?

Furthermore, I am less concerned with what one learns and *hopes* to do for a lifetime during their four years of college and more focused on how graduates *actually live* once they leave college. More specifically to *influence*, is the person having a tangible influence on society with the degree he earned? Is there production added to the world around him? Is he having a heightened impact with his degree, or could he have had the same influence by foregoing college?

Illustrating well both points, take a graduate with a degree in art history.[5] In his early to mid-twenties, mom and dad have told him that he needs to move out and get a job—start his life. So he moves out and starts looking for a job. However, with one of the highest unemployment and underemployment rates in higher education today, it is likely that this person will not be entering a career in a field related to his degree—studying history, restoring art, teaching the world around him about the subject. Instead, it is all too common for this person to find only a low-level service job, which does not demand a college education, making the minimum wage or close to it.

Barely able to make ends meet, he is forced to pick up a second job and extra hours once his student loan bills start arriving six months later. This graduate quickly finds himself on a human guinea pig wheel. No matter how hard he tries to work his way out from underneath the massive debt that he has incurred, it is insurmountable. He will spend the rest of his life struggling to emerge from the abyss of debt, working one low-level job to the next just to survive.

The harsh reality facing this person is that after spending large sums of time and money to study and develop a passion for art history in college, he will have neither the time nor the money to apply those skills for professional or personal benefit. When one has to work two full-time jobs just to make ends meet, there is no time or money left over to visit an art museum so that he may appreciate the paintings and sculptures with his newfound knowledge, or to travel the world and witness firsthand the art and architecture he studied. Ultimately, his time in college was completed in vain. After years of enduring this fight for survival, the wealth of knowledge and spirit that he once had as a young graduate has been slowly beaten out of him and reduced to nothing.

In addition to not benefiting from the personal wealth gained from a college degree—in both a monetary and personal fulfillment sense— the public investment in subsidizing this degree is also being squandered. In 2014, the federal government issued approximately $134 billion in aid to students, whether through Direct Stafford Loans, Pell Grants, Direct PLUS Loans, Perkins Loans, and so on.[6] If it were not for the federal government subsidizing higher education, most college students today could not afford it.

Thinking back to our earlier discussion of the NDEA, the initiative of making higher education affordable to the masses did not have an objective of facilitating personal amusement or fulfillment. In the early spirit of George Washington's proposed National University, higher education subsidies were intended to benefit the public, to strengthen the collective body as a nation. To the point of *wealth* and *influence* in a public sense, the purpose of early higher education subsidies to the masses was to: (1) strengthen the economy, (2) improve innovation, and (3) ensure national security. This is achieved largely in two regards.

First to *wealth*, higher wages grant consumers more purchasing power. With higher salaries that are generally associated with careers as professionals, people have more money to spend on goods and services, thus stimulating the economy with more private spending from a robust middle class. With higher wages, more people can afford to eat out at restaurants, buy luxury and entertainment products, take vacations— ultimately causing a positive ripple effect throughout the entire economy as a result. Additionally, by the very nature of earnings, the higher your salary, the more taxable income you have. If more people are earning higher wages as professionals—able to pursue professional careers with a practical college degree—there is more tax revenue collected and, therefore, available to subsidize higher education for future generations.

Second to *influence*, aside from the greater wealth distributed in the form of more spending by consumers and larger tax pools on higher-paying salaries, the skills that people learn in college ought to translate into practical use that brings utility and increased production to society. In other words, we should expect efficiency in the system to maximize the influence of the public investment with the goal of specialization. Why train someone in anthropology just to have them work in telecommunications, transferring only the claimed "soft skills" of the degree?

Put another way, it would be like sending a medical student to law school. Sure, there are soft skills like critical thinking, writing, and communication that could be translated from a law degree to medicine, but the core functions of a doctor are found in medicine, not law. A model that promotes hopping from one field to the next lacks the focus necessary for specialization, ultimately fulfilling Wayland's fear of a model with "superficial" and "diluted" degrees that leave graduates expert in nothing.[7]

The great economic philosopher and founding visionary of capitalism, Adam Smith, establishes the importance of specialization under what is known as the "division of labor." The opening lines of his *Wealth of Nations* suggests, "The greatest improvement in the productive powers of labour, and the greater part of the skill, dexterity, and judgment with which it is anywhere directed, or applied, seem to have been the effects of the division of labour."[8]

Proposing that work should be broken up into branches, suggesting that no one person could do all of the work himself, Smith points to three reasons that account for greater productivity under specialization: (1) increase of dexterity from doing things repeatedly, (2) savings of time in passing from one task to another, and (3) the focused worker invents and innovates more.[9] To the third point in particular, Smith suggests, "It is naturally to be expected, therefore, that some one or other of those who are employed in each particular branch of labour should soon find out easier and readier methods of performing their own particular work, wherever the nature of it admits of such improvement."[10]

This mentality, although first mastered on a broad scale with the assembly line, is still applicable in a less industrial but far more global sense today. In the ever-growing and specializing global market of finance and technological innovation, our competitors have embraced specialization while the United States clings to a centuries-old higher education model founded in the generic liberal arts curriculum.

Defenders of a universal liberal arts degree for all in higher education spread a romantic notion of its effects. It describes incoming freshmen as catachrestic caterpillars who, over the course of their studies, metamorphose into brilliant butterflies that flutter off into the sunset happily ever after upon graduation—damning those who do not as dull simpletons who are unable to function in the world around them.

Frank Guido, a Culinary Institute student from Rochester, New York, endorsed this position when he went on record with the *Atlantic* to say that "people without a liberal-arts background really have no place to go with their skill sets."[11] He concluded, "They lack an overall knowledge, and an ability to relate to people and make educated decisions, and not jump to conclusions."[12] Michael Sperling, the vice president for academic affairs at the Culinary Institute, added that "there's a certain level of anti-intellectualism in the popular culture that inappropriately sees the pursuit of core disciplines as frivolous. And that's unfortunate, because the kind of things you learn in philosophy courses and history courses deepens your ability to act in the world."[13]

Some go on to cite qualitative reports with responses from employers, claiming that employers even prefer liberal arts studies to practical degrees. In a survey of 318 corporate leaders conducted by the Association of American Colleges and Universities, 93 percent supposedly agree that "a demonstrated capacity to think critically, communicate clearly, and solve complex problems" is more important than a job candidate's undergraduate major.[14]

Despite the supposed demand in liberal arts degrees, hiring statistics paint a far different picture. For an overwhelming majority of graduates, a high demand for a degree in the liberal arts is not the reality. Why? One explanation possibly rests in the notion that practical degrees might also have the ability to teach problem solving and communication skills in addition to the core skills of whatever field it might be.

If a machine breaks down, for example, the person who fixes it does not debate the machine back to working with Socratic rhetoric. He solves the mechanical problem of whatever broke the machine. He is able to communicate and problem-solve well enough to fix the machine. Why should we, instead, teach him to think philosophically about the purpose and feelings of machines—an art that, although creative, does not equip him with the skills to fix it?

Of course, there are exceptions to the rule and some graduates with degrees in these fields will go on to be successful in such areas of study—and I commend them for it. My comments here are in no way a critique of the academic merits of liberal arts, but simply to report that the volume of them is too great at the present time as determined by the job market. In other words, where and when liberal arts degrees translate into sustaining and productive jobs, they ought to be celebrated and promoted. But where and when those degrees, along with any degree type for that matter, fail to bring the tangible promise of sustainable earnings and production to the individual and society, they ought to be condemned and eliminated.

With this said, liberal arts will survive and flourish in certain settings. Some colleges are better than others, whether by the caliber of students they attract or the professors that lead them in their studies. It would not be fair to single out any one institution, but there can be no comparison between the quality of the education at a top tier university and that of an institution ranked 700th, much less 7,000th. By the natural sifting process that occurs during application and admission, the vast majority of our nation's brightest minds attend the top colleges and universities, not an institution buried on the twentieth page of the national rankings.

Those who have the capacity to think most exceptionally—critically, broadly, with agility—these are the people who have the potential to lead a fulfilling life with a career in these fields that will help change the world we live in. What is wrong is to pretend that everyone can and will measure up to this standard, for when we do, there is a great disservice done to both the individual and society alike.

In the words of Frank Underwood, "There is nothing left of the farm, which is for the best. The peaches didn't want to grow here anyways. That's what you get for planting on land with solid rock two feet beneath the top soil. . . . Hard work is only worth it in the right conditions."[15] For all of his faults, the fictional character of the Netflix series hit *House of Cards* makes a critically important point. While all institutions, degrees, and minds are not created equal, everyone does have the capacity to lead a fulfilling life, as a contributing member of society with an education under the right conditions.

Society is comprised of a robust and diverse job market, where everyone from doctors to dairy farmers requires varying degrees of educational time and substance as they specialize toward becoming practitioners. How can a single model based upon liberal arts possibly satisfy the needs of each of these career paths? Sure, problem solving and communication are important and they sound official, but the core material of each is vastly different. Moreover, practical-centered curriculum is not blind to skills like problem solving and communication. Those skills are simply more focused and purposefully tailored to whatever area of study the student pursues.

Aside from the debate over the value and restrictive realities of a broad liberal arts higher education model, there is an additional argument that a college degree is neither necessary nor appropriate to create a well-rounded society—the primary argument for a liberal arts higher education. In terms of its comparative education structure, the United States is an outlier from an overwhelming majority of its competitors abroad.

There are two primary elements that contribute to this outlier status: (1) the availability and curriculum of primary and secondary education, and (2) the freedom to continue on an educational path without selective barriers through mandatory benchmark examinations that place students on different education tracks.

To the former, the United States offers compulsory education to every person through the twelfth grade, otherwise known as primary and secondary education. During this education, students are enrolled in a series of core competency subjects (math, science, English, and social studies), in addition to having widespread access to electives that allow students to further explore their interests and creative capacity. These electives include but are not limited to courses in business, computer science/information technology, family/consumer science, foreign language, language and writing, performing arts, physical education, and visual arts. [16]

To the latter, the United States grants access to the same education for all of its students throughout their primary and secondary years, as well as the open opportunity to apply for college despite their aptitude as indicated by standardized exams. According to a study filed in the European Parliament, while the United States has a "unitary system in upper secondary education which accommodates students regardless of their aptitude levels," countries like "Germany, France, Italy and Japan have different school types for students of different aptitudes, typically separated between an academic and a vocational track." [17]

Elaborating on the system of selective placement into different tracks of education, many countries begin to funnel students into different tracks as early as fifth or sixth grade, and a majority solidify these classifications by tenth grade.[18] In Germany, after *Grundschule*, primary education for grades 1–4, placement exams roughly at the age of ten direct students into either *Hauptschule*, *Realschule*, or *Gymnasium*.[19]

While *Hauptschule* holds the lowest-performing students that are set on tracks for vocational training and specialization, *Realschule* provides students with an education that combines both liberal and practical education from the fifth through the tenth grade.[20] The education focus of *Realschule* is differentiated between the *Unterstufe* (lower level), which incorporates the fifth, sixth, and seventh grades, and the *Oberstufe* (upper level), which includes the eighth, ninth, and tenth grades.[21] Finally, *Gymnasium* provides the highest-performing students with a liberal education and traditionally leads to study at the university.[22]

The purpose of this comparison is to demonstrate that the United States is progressive in its commitment to providing a liberal arts education and promoting a well-rounded society well before the college level. There are few countries in the world that mandate compulsory education through the twelfth grade equivalent, and even fewer grant the entire student population the opportunity to read *Hamlet*, perform an instrument, and engage with civics.

By international standards, our education structure provides the general populace with the opportunity to be well read and well exposed to a vast array of studies through early adulthood. Such exposure has led the United States to generate one of the most well-rounded populations in the world that is sufficient for people to lead enlightened and fulfilling lives as contributing members of society.

Critics, however, might rightfully question the reality of the real well-roundedness of high school graduates, pointing to inconsistent funding across districts and a recent movement to graduate low-performing students for the sake of meeting federal mandates and satisfying public demand for better student outcomes. The *New York Times* suggested that this is a growing pattern, "where the number of students earning high school diplomas has risen to historic peaks, yet measures of academic readiness for college or jobs are much lower," adding that "this has led educators to question the real value of a high school diploma and whether graduation requirements are too easy."[23]

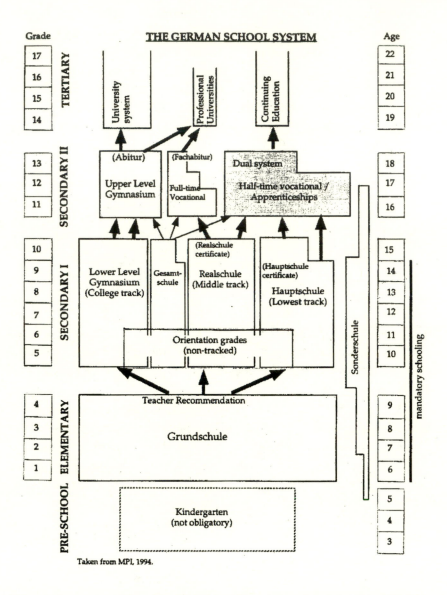

Taken from MPI, 1994.

Figure 9.1.   German Education Model.   *Source: Milwaukee Public Library, 1994. Cited by http://facstaff.bloomu.edu/lspringm/resources/schulsystem.html.*

The *New York Times* editorial board went to add that "less than 40 percent of 12th graders are ready for math and reading at the college level" and that a study conducted by the Education Trust, a nonpartisan foundation, found that "more than one in five recent high school graduates could not meet minimum entry test standards to enlist in the Army."[24]

Based upon these figures, some would reasonably argue that many high school students can barely spell *Hamlet,* much less understand, interpret, and be influenced by it. In other words, primary and secondary education is broken and failing many of its students, and therefore cannot be propped up as the system that will bring well-roundedness to society. While this is a valid criticism, offering four years of a liberal arts education on the back end of a broken system is hardly a reasonable solution. If a twelfth-grader is reading and writing at a sixth grade level, how can we possibly expect him to perform well in college, no matter how prestigious the institution is?

Aside from the fact that it fails logically to add four years of liberal arts on the back end of a broken secondary education system, the greater point is that the structure to create a well-rounded society in primary and secondary education is already in place. The proper solution is to fix the system, not throw a wet Band-Aid on it after a decade of broken learning and call it a day.

Critics might further contend that the K–12 model ought to be extended into higher education regardless, suggesting that if I have endorsed universal liberal arts for K–12 education, there is no justification to arbitrarily end it upon completion of the secondary level. There are, however, several reasonable responses to that contention.

The first is that as a society, we have already answered this question. Our nation has decided that compulsory education, meaning a level of universal education necessary to ensure that individuals are able to function in society, is appropriate at the secondary level, nothing more. It is worth restating that the scope of this universal, secondary liberal arts education is unparalleled in the world in regard to its broad access and sophisticated curriculum.

Second, there is a classic slippery-slope dilemma in the logic that we must continue to extend this threshold with future generations. Two hundred years ago, compulsory primary education was a radical idea. One hundred fifty years ago, society began to deem it essential. One hundred years ago, this logic was extended to secondary education. Fifty years ago, the first initiatives to extend the same logic to higher education began. Twenty years ago, society regarded an associate's degree to be crucial. Today, an associate's degree is considered to be irrelevant in most circles, we hold a bachelor's degree to the same level of importance an associate's degree once held, and there are even cases where a master's degree is now required. The question is, *when does it stop?*

Over time, society has set itself on an exponential trend of never-ending educational attainment. Two hundred years ago, many people could barely read. One hundred fifty years ago, we began to universally establish basic reading, writing, and math skills. One hundred years ago, we extended the scope of this proficiency with exposure to subjects like history, algebra, and literature. In the modern era, society has broadened this exposure to an even-more-heightened level of a two-year, and eventually a four-year, college degree. *When does it stop?*

To think in other terms, two hundred years ago some people never had any years of formal educational training. One hundred fifty years ago, we established universal education to children. One hundred years ago, we extended it to teenagers. Fifty years ago, we extended it to the early twenties. Today, there is a push to extend this into our mid-twenties. *When does it stop?* If we continue upon this trend, people will be attending college universally into their thirties by the end of the century. Are we to expect that in a matter of a few generations not so far in the distant future, society will demand that everyone universally obtain doctoral degrees?

This rhetorical analysis suggests that there must be a balance. All too often does the pendulum of American policy swing from one extreme to the next, never stopping in the middle. Does universal education improve society? Yes. Does exposure to different subjects and perspectives leave people more capable to function in the world around them? Of course. However, can we reasonably continue to perpetually deem the levels of universal education today to be insufficient for tomorrow? No.

We must not confuse the appropriate functions of compulsory education and higher education. In the end, compulsory primary and secondary education creates, or ought to create, well-rounded citizens, while higher education serves the function of specialization. This does not mean specialization necessarily in a vocational sense, rather, specialization of education in general. Whether it is women's studies or welding, the nature and ultimate purpose of higher education is to master a subject, while compulsory education is to ensure exposure and well-roundedness to a variety of subjects.

In other words, a liberal arts model that exposes everyone to a variety of subjects and promotes well-roundedness is a model that should be embraced and celebrated. However, we have a structure in place at the primary and secondary levels to facilitate these goals, and to extend them broadly into higher education with no limits undermines the specialization objectives of a sustainable higher education system that strengthens the nation.

Many academics reject this philosophy, however. They view higher education and the job market itself through an elitist lens, pedestalizing the liberal arts as sacred while scoffing at vocational training as being inferior. Enthralled with their own purist view on education, those who defend a universal liberal arts model blissfully ignore the challenges graduates face in their crusade to prop up liberal arts at the expense of practical education. This position is ultimately misguided, because in the end, all higher education and all learning is nothing more and nothing less than a trade. Just because a student learns how to think one way by getting a political science degree to eventually go on to law school does not diminish another's learning in mechanical studies and then going on to become a mechanic.

We prop up doctors and lawyers as being superior in the hierarchy of society, but when did these professions become more than simply the trades of medicine and law? In the Robin Williams classic *Patch Adams*, the lead character, a young medical student testing the boundaries of treatment and patient care in the medical field, alludes to this very point: "Is not a doctor someone who helps someone else? When did the term *doctor* get treated with such reverence. . . . At what point in history did a doctor become more than a trusted and learned friend who visited and treated the ill?"[25]

This same philosophy ought to be applied universally. The value of higher education cannot emphasize one form of study over another merely by the content. In the end, we are all learning a trade, no matter what that trade might be. Lawyers learn the trade of law, just as welders learn the trade of crafting metal. We all learn how to think, how to problem-solve, and how to bring value to the world around us with specialized skills that come from our higher education. The only differentiating factor is the varying degree of success people have in applying that trade in the job market as a profession.

Regardless of what critics might say about the philosophy that has been expressed throughout this chapter, it is important to continually return to the question—what is the purpose of higher education? Equally if not more important than the question of purpose is the question of sustainability and how to reconcile the two. There may be a fierce debate over the former, but there is no discussion for the latter. As John Adams famously once said, "Facts are stubborn things; and whatever may be our wishes, our inclinations, or the dictates of our passion, they cannot alter the state of facts and evidence."[26]

It is an undeniable fact that our national student loan debt has already surpassed $1.3 trillion, and continues to grow at $2,726 every second.[27] This means that the student debt continues to climb at $163,560 per minute, $9.8 million per hour, $235.5 million per day, $1.6 billion per week, $6.6 billion per month, and approximately $86 billion per year.

To put this figure into perspective, our student debt is approximately the same size as the gross domestic product (GDP) of Spain, Mexico, South Korea, and Australia, all of which are holding roughly $1.3 trillion and considered to be among the top fifteen wealthiest nations on Earth.[28] On this trajectory, the national student debt is expected to surpass $1.5 trillion in 2017 and $2 trillion by 2022, matching the nominal GDP of Italy, India, and Brazil, which are considered to be among the top ten wealthiest countries in the world.

If the point has not been made clear enough yet, then the simple way of saying it is that our system of higher education is unequivocally unsustainable in its current form. Continuing upon a path that mindlessly titillates people's fantasies, hobbies, and comforts with no regard to its long-term costs will ultimately serve as the chopping block of our own demise. Whatever we choose to adopt in the years ahead, it cannot be a system as it exists today. We can no longer afford to go on with our heads floating in the clouds or buried in the sand.

ESSENTIAL TAKEAWAYS AND FINAL THOUGHTS

The great paradox of the college affordability crisis is that we can be forward-looking only after returning to the original mission of subsidizing higher education for millions of Americans as a way to strengthen the economy, improve innovation, and ensure national security.

Although some would argue that this is already the case in higher education today, reality illustrates a far different picture. Whether it is the wasteful spending on unnecessary amenities in the perpetual arms race between institutions or the blatant disregard for job market demand, the status quo is far from achieving that original mission. So much of higher education is infatuated with amusing students, whether with lavish dining halls or entertaining yet practically useless studies.

These observations raise an interesting point made by Benjamin Rush, who said, "To spend four or five years in learning two dead languages, is to turn our backs upon a gold mine, in order to amuse ourselves catching butterflies."[29] Although today's colleges and universities do not offer the same "stultifying, unimaginative, and inadequate" curriculum of two dead languages, its practical worth or lack thereof serves students as if it did.[30]

Sure, students may feel a sense of temporary personal fulfillment while they are enrolled in college and learning about less practical fields, but once they leave, many depart out into the world with no tangible assets that benefit them or society. As a Harvard commencement orator in 1677 observed, "Mad nobodies, haranguers at street-corners, have more influence with the populace than reverent men, filled with singular gifts of the divine spirit."[31]

As our swelling national student debt shows no signs of subsiding, the bubble will inevitably burst if the inefficiencies of the status quo go uncorrected. With the purpose of avoiding such an event, I believe that the proposals that have been made throughout this book not only have the potential of saving millions of Americans from the continuing trend of financial ruin, but also will help to prevent the looming financial collapse that our country faces if we do nothing.

We are at a crossroads as a nation, and there are steps that can be taken to fix the escalating problem before it is too late. Although we are not sure of exactly how extreme the consequences of inaction will be if the college financial bubble bursts, we can be certain that this approaching catastrophe is not too far off in the distant future. Let us change this trend of the college affordability crisis before we reach our breaking point.

NOTES

INTRODUCTION

1. William J. Bennett, "The Looming Crisis of Student Loan Debt," *CNN*, December 6, 2012, www.cnn.com/2012/12/06/opinion/bennett-student-debt (accessed August 19, 2013).

2. National Center for Education Statistics, "Table 320: Average Undergraduate Tuition and Fees and Room and Board Rates Charged for Full-Time Students in Degree-Granting Institutions, by Type and Control of Institution: 1964–65 through 2006–07," U.S. Department of Education Institute of Education Sciences, 2008, https://nces.ed.gov/programs/digest/d07/tables/dt07_320.asp (accessed February 20, 2016); Travis Mitchell, "See 20 Years of Tuition Growth at National Universities," *U.S. News & World Report*, July 29, 2015, www.usnews.com/education/best-colleges/paying-for-college/articles/2015/07/29/chart-see-20-years-of-tuition-growth-at-national-universities (accessed February 20, 2016).

3. Adam Levin, "Is College Tuition the Next Bubble?," *ABC News*, March 24, 2012, http://abcnews.go.com/Business/bubble-time-cap-college-tuition/story?id=15987539 (accessed August 20, 2013).

4. Bennett, "The Looming Crisis of Student Loan Debt."

5. Jeffrey Sparshott, "Congratulations, Class of 2015. You're the Most Indebted Ever (for Now)," May 8, 2015, http://blogs.wsj.com/economics/2015/05/08/congratulations-class-of-2015-youre-the-most-indebted-ever-for-now (accessed May 10, 2015).

6. Suzanne Mettler, *Degrees of Inequality: How the Politics of Higher Education Sabotaged the American Dream* (New York: Basic Books, 2014), 4.

7. Ibid., 5.

8. Robert Samuelson, "It's Time to Drop the College-for-All Crusade," *Washington Post*, May 27, 2012, www.washingtonpost.com/opinions/its-time-to-drop-the-college-for-all-crusade/2012/05/27/gJQAzcUGvU_story.html (accessed March 30, 2014).

1. SOWING THE SEEDS OF CRISIS

1. Frederick Rudolph, *The American College and University: A History* (New York: Alfred A. Knopf, 1962), 3.

2. Samuel Eliot Morison, *Harvard College in the Seventeenth Century* (Cambridge: Harvard University Press, 1936), 536.

3. Rudolph, *The American College and University*, 6.

4. Ibid., 16.

5. Herbert Baxter Adams, *The College of William and Mary* (Washington, DC: GPO, 1887), 21, http://catalog.hathitrust.org/Record/001452367 (accessed March 24, 2014).

6. Rudolph, *The American College and University*, 19.

7. Morison, *Harvard College in the Seventeenth Century*, 61.

8. Rudolph, *The American College and University*, 20.

9. Ibid., 20–21.

10. Ibid., 20.

11. Ibid., 22.

12. Ibid., 34.

13. Ibid., 35–36.

14. Kemp Plummer Battle, *History of the University of North Carolina*, vol. 1 (Raleigh, NC: Edwards & Broughton, 1907), 2.

15. Rudolph, *The American College and University*, 41.

16. Allen Oscar Hansen, *Liberalism and American Education in the Eighteenth Century* (New York: The Macmillan Company, 1926), 105.

17. Rudolph, *The American College and University*, 47.

18. Donald George Tewksbury, *The Founding of American Colleges and Universities Before the Civil War* (Mansfield Center, CT: Martino Fine Books, 2011), 3.

19. Rudolph, *The American College and University: A History*, 48–49.

20. Roger L. Williams, *Origins of Federal Support for Higher Education: George W. Atherton and the Land-Grant College Movement* (University Park: Pennsylvania State University Press, 1991), 13.

21. Ibid.

22. Ibid., 14.

23. Rudolph, *The American College and University*, 202.

24. Kevin Kinser, *From Main Street to Wall Street: The Transformation of For-Profit Higher Education* (San Francisco, CA: Jossey-Bass, 2006), 17.

25. Rudolph, *The American College and University*, 202.

26. Ibid.

27. Williams, *Origins of Federal Support for Higher Education*, 15.

28. Ibid.

29. Ibid.

30. Rudolph, *The American College and University*, 21.

31. Williams, *Origins of Federal Support for Higher Education*, 15.

32. Michael S. Katz, *A History of Compulsory Education Laws, U.S. Department of Health, Education and Welfare National Institute of Education* (Bloomington, IN: Phi Delta Kappa Educational Foundation, 1976), 17–20.

33. Williams, *Origins of Federal Support for Higher Education*, 19.

34. Kinser, *From Main Street to Wall Street*, 18.

35. C. A. Herrick, *Meaning and Practice of Commercial Education* (New York: Macmillan Co., 1904).

36. Kinser, *From Main Street to Wall Street*, 18.

37. Williams, *Origins of Federal Support for Higher Education*, 16.

38. Rudolph, *The American College and University*, 264.

39. Ibid., 51–52.

40. Ibid., 265.

41. Ibid., 58.

42. James E. Pollard, *History of the Ohio State University: The Story of Its First Seventy-Five Years* (Columbus: Ohio State University Press, 1952), 350.

43. Rudolph, *The American College and University*, 61.

44. Ibid., 65.

45. Ibid., 222.

46. Ibid.

47. Stuart S. Holland, "Hydraulic Mining Methods," British Columbia Department of Mines, Bulletin No. 15, 5, www.empr.gov.bc.ca/Mining/Geoscience/PublicationsCatalogue/BulletinInformation/BulletinsAfter1940/Documents/Bull15.pdf (accessed December 31, 2015).

48. Williams, *Origins of Federal Support for Higher Education*, 19.

49. Ibid.

50. Rudolph, *The American College and University*, 233.

51. Williams, *Origins of Federal Support for Higher Education*, 21.

52. Ibid.

53. Williams, *Origins of Federal Support for Higher Education*, 21.

54. Rudolph, *The American College and University*, 234.

55. Ibid.

56. Ibid., 236.

57. Ibid.

58. Ibid., 238.

59. Francis Wayland, *Report to the Corporation of Brown University on Changes in the System of Collegiate Education*, read March 28, 1850, 50–52.

60. Rudolph, *The American College and University*, 232.

61. Ibid., 240.

62. Jonas Viles, *The University of Missouri: A Centennial History* (Columbia: University of Missouri, 1939), 108.

63. Rudolph, *The American College and University*, 332.

64. Claudia Goldin and Lawrence F. Katz, "The Shaping of Higher Education: The Formative Years in the United States, 1890-1940," *Journal of Economic Perspectives* 13, no. 1 (1999): 37, http://faculty.smu.edu/millimet/classes/eco4361/readings/goldin%20katz%201999.pdf (accessed January 3, 2016).

65. Ibid., 37–38.

66. Ibid., 38.

67. Ibid., 39.

68. Grant Venn, *Man, Education and Work: Postsecondary Vocational and Technical Education* (Washington DC: American Council on Education, 1964).

69. Digest of Education Statistics, "Table 303.10. Total Fall Enrollment in Degree-Granting Postsecondary Institutions, by Attendance Status, Sex of Student, and Control of Institution: Selected Years, 1947 through 2023," National Center for Education Statistics, 2013, http://nces.ed.gov/programs/digest/d13/tables/dt13_303.10.asp (accessed January 1, 2016).

70. Ibid.

71. Suzanne Mettler, *Degrees of Inequality: How the Politics of Higher Education Sabotaged the American Dream* (New York: Basic Books, 2014), 4.

72. Mark Gongloff, "Why You Should Really Go to College, in 2 Charts," *Huffington Post*, February 20, 2015, www.huffingtonpost.com/2015/02/20/college-income-premium_n_6720902.html (accessed January 3, 2016).

73. Rudolph, *The American College and University*, 21.

2. TANKED BY RANK

1. NCSL: National Conference of State Legislatures, "For-Profit Colleges and Universities," July 2013, www.ncsl.org/research/education/for-profit-colleges-and-universities.aspx (accessed December 5, 2013).

2. Community College Research Center, "Community College Enrollment and Completion," 2012, http://ccrc.tc.columbia.edu/Community

-College-FAQs.html (accessed January 3, 2014).

3. Digest of Education Statistics, "Table 303.10. Total Fall Enrollment in Degree-Granting Postsecondary Institutions, by Attendance Status, Sex of Student, and Control of Institution: Selected Years, 1947 through 2023," National Center for Education Statistics, 2013, http://nces.ed.gov/programs/digest/d13/tables/dt13_303.10.asp (accessed January 1, 2016).

4. National Center for Education Statistics, "Table 320: Average Undergraduate Tuition and Fees and Room and Board Rates Charged for Full-Time Students in Degree-Granting Institutions, by Type and Control of Institution: 1964–65 through 2006–07," U.S. Department of Education Institute of Education Sciences, 2008, https://nces.ed.gov/programs/digest/d07/tables/dt07_320.asp (accessed February 20, 2016); Travis Mitchell, "See 20 Years of Tuition Growth at National Universities," *U.S. News & World Report*, July 29, 2015, www.usnews.com/education/best-colleges/paying-for-college/articles/2015/07/29/chart-see-20-years-of-tuition-growth-at-national-universities (accessed February 20, 2016).

5. Ibid.

6. Jillian Berman, "Watch America's Student-Loan Debt Grow $2,726 Every Second," *Market Watch*, January 30, 2016, www.marketwatch.com/story/every-second-americans-get-buried-under-another-3055-in-student-loan-debt-2015-06-10 (accessed January 31, 2016).

7. Jeffrey Sparshott, "Congratulations, Class of 2015. You're the Most Indebted Ever (for Now)," blog, May 8, 2015, http://blogs.wsj.com/economics/2015/05/08/congratulations-class-of-2015-youre-the-most-indebted-ever-for-now (accessed May 10, 2015).

8. IMF World Economic Outlook (WEO), October 2015, http://knoema.com/nwnfkne/world-gdp-ranking-2015-data-and-charts (accessed January 30, 2016).

9. Jonathan Robe, "The Race for Prestige Drives College Costs," Forbes Contributed through CCAP, October 10, 2011, www.forbes.com/sites/ccap/2011/10/10/the-race-for-prestige-drives-college-costs (accessed December 18, 2013).

10. Ronald G. Ehrenberg, *Tuition Rising: Why College Costs So Much* (Cambridge: Harvard University Press, 2002), 16.

11. "An Inquiry in the Rising Cost of Higher Education: Summary of Responses from Seventy College and University Presidents," Davis Educational Foundation, November 2012, 2, www.google.com/url?sa=t&rct=j&q=&esrc=s&frm=1&source=web&cd=1&ved=0CCwQFjAA&url=http%3A%2F%2Fwww.davisfoundations.org%2Fsite%2Fdocuments%2FAnInquiryintotheRisingCostofHigherEducation_003.pdf&ei=fRnJUtfoBNbJsQS1

-ILoDQ&usg=AFQjCNFK6edk9Ifw6wMhSFJBxO7MiouWIw&sig2
=B9V46319Ra28rnzcTA096A (accessed January 1, 2014).

12. Ehrenberg, *Tuition Rising*, supra note table 4.2, at 54.

13. Robert Morse and Eric Brooks, "Best Colleges Ranking Criteria and Weights," *U.S. News and World Report*, September 8, 2015, www.usnews.com/education/best-colleges/articles/ranking-criteria-and-weights (accessed December 19, 2015).

14. Ibid.

15. Ibid.

16. Ibid.

17. Ehrenberg, *Tuition Rising*, 58.

18. "An Inquiry in the Rising Cost of Higher Education," 3.

19. Sandy Baum, Charles Kurose, and Michael McPherson, "An Overview of American Higher Education," *The Future of Children* 23, no. 1 (2013): 32–33.

20. Yasumi Abe and Satoshi P. Watanabe, "Academic Crossover and Functional Differentiation of Universities," Research Institute for Higher Education, July 27, 2012, 338.

21. Ehrenberg, *Tuition Rising*, 26.

22. Bill Destler, "Competition and the Rising Cost of Higher Education," *Huffington Post*, September 10, 2012, www.huffingtonpost.com/bill-destler/college-competition-_b_1867165.html?view=print&comm_ref=false (accessed December 20, 2013).

23. Ehrenberg, *Tuition Rising*, 60. As *USN&WR* indicates, "We are measuring financial resources by the average spending per student on instruction, research, public service, academic support, student services, institutional support, and operations and maintenance."

24. Ehrenberg, *Tuition Rising*, 146.

25. Jeff Denneen and Tom Dretler, "The Financially Sustainable University," Bain & Company, 2012, 3, www.bain.com/publications/articles/financially-sustainable-university.aspx (accessed January 4, 2014).

26. Ehrenberg, *Tuition Rising*, 149.

27. Ibid.

28. Paul Abramson, "2013 College Construction Report: Proceeding with Caution," Peter Li Education Group: College Planning & Management, February 2013, 2, www.peterli.com/cpm/pdfs/CollegeConstructionReport2013 (accessed December 20, 2013). College Planning & Management works in conjunction with Market Data Retrieval (MDR), a company of Dun and Bradstreet (D&B). MDR contacts two-year and four-year colleges and universities, public and private, throughout the United States seeking information on their

construction plans—new buildings, additions to existing buildings, major reno-
vations, and retrofitting projects.

29. Ibid.

30. Anirban Basu, "Higher Education Construction Spending: Peak, Slump,
Recover?," *Construction Executive: The Magazine for Business Construction*,
June 2011, www.constructionexec.com/Issues/June_2011/Economic
_Outlook.aspx (accessed January 1, 2014).

31. Abramson, "2013 College Construction Report," 2.

32. Donna M. Desrochers and Rita J. Kirshstein, "College Spending in a
Turbulent Decade: Findings from the Delta Cost Project," American Institutes
for Research (AIR): A Delta Data Update 2000–2010, 3, www.air.org/
expertise/index/?fa=viewContent&content_id=2200 (accessed December 20,
2013).

33. Ibid.

34. Abramson, "2013 College Construction Report," 2.

35. Kim Clark, "Tuition at Public Colleges Rises 4.8%," *CNN Money*, October 24, 2012, http://money.cnn.com/2012/10/24/pf/college/public-college
-tuition (accessed January 8, 2014).

36. Ronald Ehrenberg and Ross Milton, "The Other Debt Crisis," *Cornell
Alumni Magazine*, December 2013, 48.

37. Kate Gibson, "Wall Street Closes 2013 at Records; Best Year in 16 for
S&P, 18 for Dow," *CNBC: US Markets*, December 31, 2013, www.cnbc.com/
id/101303244 (accessed January 1, 2014).

38. Ylan Q. Mui, "U.S. Economy Adds 203,000 Jobs November; Unemployment Rate Down to 7 Percent," *Washington Post: Business*, December 6,
2013, www.washingtonpost.com/business/economy/economy-added-203k-
jobs-in-november-unemployment-down-to-7percent/2013/12/06/a183a50c-
5dfa-11e3-bc56-c6ca94801fac_story.html (accessed January 1, 2014).

39. Lu Wang and Callie Bost, "U.S. Stocks Rise to Records as GDP Growth
Tops Estimates," *Bloomberg News*, December 20, 2013, www.bloomberg.com/
news/2013-12-20/u-s-stock-index-futures-rise-as-red-hat-carnival-gain.html
(accessed January 1, 2014).

3. PENNILESS FOR PERKS

1. Paul Abramson, "2013 College Construction Report: Proceeding with
Caution," Peter Li Education Group: College Planning & Management, February 2013, 6, www.peterli.com/cpm/pdfs/CollegeConstructionReport2013
(accessed December 20, 2013).

2. Paul Abramson, "2007 College Construction Report," Peter Li Education Group: College Planning & Management, February 2007, graph A, 6, www.peterli.com/global/pdfs/CPMConstruction2007 (accessed December 20, 2013).

3. Paul Abramson, "2013 College Construction Report: Proceeding with Caution," 6.

4. Abramson, "2007 College Construction Report," graph B, 7.

5. Ibid., graph C, 7.

6. Ibid., graph D, 7.

7. "An Inquiry in the Rising Cost of Higher Education: Summary of Responses from Seventy College and University Presidents," Davis Educational Foundation, 1.

8. Ibid., 3.

9. Ibid. On the note that families have "less to spend," the report describes that "the problem is the Federal Reserve reports an inflation-adjusted median family income decline of 7.6 percent between 2007 and 2010 and a median family net worth decline of 39 percent. Rising student debt levels further demonstrate the persistent disequilibrium between net tuitions and student ability to pay for college. The poor job market makes servicing student debt upon graduation extremely difficult and default rates are increasing."

10. Brian Jacob, Brian McCall, and Kevin M. Strange, *College as Country Club: Do Colleges Cater to Students' Preferences for Consumption?* (Cambridge: National Bureau of Economic Research, 2013), 7.

11. Ibid., 11.

12. Ibid., 22. Table 2 on page 51 offers the specific characteristics of students that were tested, as well as their preferences.

13. Ibid., 19.

14. Ibid., 20.

15. Ibid.

16. Ibid., 25.

17. Ibid., 26. Figure F1 in the appendix presents the distribution of WTP from the model without college fixed effects. In this model, the qualitative finding that the WTP for marginal changes in consumption amenities is greater (more positive) than that for instruction still holds: all students have a positive WTP for consumption amenities, but only a small percentage do for instructional spending, though the scale differs.

18. Ibid., 33.

19. Ibid., 37.

20. Ronald G. Ehrenberg, *Tuition Rising: Why College Costs So Much* (Cambridge: Harvard University Press, 2002), 146.

21. Sam Dillon, "Share of College Spending for Recreation Is Rising," *New York Times*, July 9, 2010, www.nytimes.com/2010/07/10/education/10education.html?_r=0 (accessed December 22, 2013).

22. Matthew Segal, "How Colleges Are Complicit in Raising Tuition," *CNN Money*, October 28, 2013, http://finance.fortune.cnn.com/2013/10/28/college-tuition-george-washington (accessed December 22, 2013).

23. Ibid.

24. "Summer Construction Projects Improve Campus," Penn State University, June 4, 2012, http://news.psu.edu/story/148580/2012/06/04/summer-construction-projects-improve-campus (accessed December 22, 2013).

25. Supra at p. 120.

26. Sandy Baum, Charles Kurose, and Michael McPherson, "An Overview of American Higher Education," *The Future of Children* 23, no. 1 (2013): 33.

27. Suzanne Mettler, *Degrees of Inequality: How the Politics of Higher Education Sabotaged the American Dream* (New York: Basic Books, 2014), 9.

28. "Administrative Bloat at American Universities: The Real Reason for High Costs in Higher Education," Policy Report No. 239, Goldwater Institute, August 17, 2010, 1, www.voced.edu.au/content/ngv45526 (accessed January 9, 2014).

29. Ibid., figure 5, 7.

30. Ibid., figure 6, 8.

31. Jeff Denneen and Tom Dretler, "The Financially Sustainable University," Bain & Company, 2012, 3, www.bain.com/publications/articles/financially-sustainable-university.aspx (accessed January 4, 2014).

32. "Administrative Bloat at American Universities," 8.

33. Richard Vedder, "What Do 2,358 College Administrators Do?," *Bloomberg News*, July 15, 2013, www.bloomberg.com/news/2013-07-15/napolitano-expert-in-bloated-bureaucracies.html. (accessed January 7, 2014).

34. "Administrative Bloat at American Universities," 10.

35. Ibid., 11.

36. Ibid.

37. Ibid., 13.

38. Beth Akers, "Consumption Amenities in Higher Education," Brookings Institution, February 6, 2013, www.brookings.edu/blogs/brown-center-chalkboard/posts/2013/02/06-higher-ed-costs-akers (accessed December 23, 2013).

39. Her Campus, "The 5 Craziest College Majors," *Huffington Post*, February 25, 2013, www.huffingtonpost.com/her-campus/weirdest-college-majors_b_2756529.html (accessed January 31, 2016).

40. Bowling Green State University, "Department of Popular Culture," 2016, www.bgsu.edu/arts-and-sciences/cultural-and-critical-studies/popular-culture.html (accessed January 31, 2016).

41. Plymouth State University, "Department of Adventure Education," 2016, www.plymouth.edu/department/hhp/degrees-options-minors/bs-adventure-education/what-is-adventure-education (accessed January 31, 2016).

42. Stetson University, "Department of Family Enterprise," 2016, www.stetson.edu/other/academics/programs/family-enterprise.php (accessed January 31, 2016).

43. Georgetown University, "Department of Philosophy: Philosophy of Star Trek," 2016, http://courses.georgetown.edu/?CourseID=PHIL-180 (accessed January 31, 2016).

44. University of Maryland, "American Studies: Perspectives on Identity and Culture; Introduction to Fat Studies," 2016, https://ntst.umd.edu/soc/201512/AMST/AMST328C (accessed January 31, 2016).

45. University of California at Irvine, "Physics Department: Science of Superheroes," 2016, http://ocw.uci.edu/courses/physics_21_science_from_superheroes_to_global_warming.html (accessed January 31, 2016).

46. Akers, "Consumption Amenities in Higher Education."

47. "An Inquiry in the Rising Cost of Higher Education," 4.

4. LENDING ROOTS

1. Beth Akers, "Consumption Amenities in Higher Education," Brookings Institution, February 6, 2013, www.brookings.edu/blogs/brown-center-chalkboard/posts/2013/02/06-higher-ed-costs-akers (accessed December 23, 2013).

2. Servicemen's Readjustment Act (GI Bill), Title II: Chapter IV Education of Veterans, Sec. 400 Part VIII(5), June 22, 1944. "The Administrator shall pay to the educational or training institution, for each person enrolled in full time or part time course of education or training, the customary cost of tuition, and such laboratory, library, health, infirmary, and other similar fees as are customarily charged, and may pay for books, supplies, equipment, and other necessary expenses, exclusive of board, lodging, other living expenses, and travel, as are generally required for the successful pursuit and completion of the course by other students in the institution: Provided, That in no event shall such payments, with respect to any person, exceed $500 for an ordinary school year: Provided further, That no payments shall be made to institutions, business or other establishments furnishing apprentice training on the job: And

provided further, That if any such institution has no established tuition fee, or if its established tuition fee shall be found by the Administrator to be inadequate compensation to such institution for furnishing such education or training, he is authorized to provide for the payment, with respect to any such person, of such fair and reasonable compensation as will not exceed $500 for an ordinary school year."

3. President Franklin D. Roosevelt's statement on signing the GI Bill, June 22, 1944, www.gibill.va.gov/benefits/history_timeline (accessed January 6, 2014).

4. "The GI BILL's History—Born of Controversy: The GI Bill of Rights," U.S. Department of Veterans Affairs, February 9, 2012, www.benefits.va.gov/gibill/history.asp (accessed May 1, 2016).

5. Steve Garber, "Sputnik and the Dawn of the Space Age," NASA, October 10, 2007, http://history.nasa.gov/sputnik/chronology.html (accessed May 1, 2016).

6. National Defense Education Act, Title I: General Provisions, Sec. 101, September 2, 1958, 1581.

7. Lawrence E. Gladieux and Arthur M. Hauptman, *The College Aid Quandary: Access, Quality, and the Federal Role* (Washington DC: Brookings Institution, 1995), 14.

8. National Defense Education Act, Title II: Loans to Students in Institutions of Higher Education, Sec. 205(a), September 2, 1958, 1583.

9. Samuel H. Williamson, "Seven Ways to Compute the Relative Value of a U.S. Dollar Amount, 1774 to Present," MeasuringWorth, April 2013, www.measuringworth.com/uscompare/result.php?year_source=1958&amount=655000000&year_result=2013 (accessed May 1, 2016).

10. National Defense Education Act, Title II: Loans to Students in Institutions of Higher Education, Sec. 204(a) September 2, 1958, 1584.

11. National Defense Education Act, Title II: Loans to Students in Institutions of Higher Education, Sec. 204(a,b) September 2, 1958, 1584.

12. President Lyndon B. Johnson, "The Great Society," University of Michigan, May 22, 1964, www.pbs.org/wgbh/americanexperience/features/primary-resources/lbj-michigan (accessed May 1, 2016).

13. 1940s War, Cold War and Consumerism, Advertising Age, 76(13), 2005, 38-40. Retrieved from http://adage.com/article/75-years-of-ideas/1940s-cold-war-consumerism/102702/.

14. "By the end of the decade, television was widely viewed as the medium of the future. After a promising start—RCA ran the first ad campaign for TV sets in 1940, the Federal Communications Commission approved commercial TV in 1941, and Bulova ran the first TV spot on New York's WNBT-TV in 1941—TV was effectively put on hold during the war. After the war, however,

the technology took off. RCA Victor became the first postwar manufacturer to advertise TV sets, in 1946, and household penetration quickly rose from 0.5% in 1948 to more than one-third of homes in 1952."

15. *October Sky*, directed by Joe Johnston, Universal Studios, released February 19, 1999.

16. Becky Bradley, "American Cultural History," Lone Star College–Kingwood, 1998.

5. SALLIE MAE

1. Congressional Budget Office, *Controlling the Risks of Government-Sponsored Enterprises* (Washington DC: U.S. Government Printing Office, 1991), 249.

2. Sallie Mae, *The Restructuring of Sallie Mae: Rationale and Feasibility*, March 1994, 1.

3. Ibid.

4. CBO, *Controlling the Risks of Government-Sponsored Enterprises*, 242.

5. Department of the Treasury, "Lessons Learned from the Privatization of Sallie Mae," Office of Sallie Mae Oversight, March 2006, 71, www.treasury.gov/about/organizational-structure/offices/Documents/SallieMaePrivatizationReport.pdf (accessed May 2, 2016).

6. Ibid.

7. Subcommittee on Postsecondary Education, Committee on Education and Labor, U.S. House of Representatives, 96th Congress, 1st Session, 1979 (testimony of Alfred B. Fitt, General Counsel, Congressional Budget Office), May 30, 1979, 11.

8. Thomas H. Stanton, "The Privatization of Sallie Mae and Its Consequences," American Enterprise Institute, June 26, 2007, 6, www.aei.org/events/the-privatization-of-sallie-mae-and-its-consequences (accessed May 2, 2016).

9. CBO, Sallie Mae, and USA Education, Inc., annual financial statements, 1991.

10. Stanton, "The Privatization of Sallie Mae and Its Consequences," 7.

11. Ibid.

12. CBO, Sallie Mae, and USA Education, Inc., annual financial statements, 1991.

13. CBO, *Controlling the Risks of Government-Sponsored Enterprises*, 249.

14. Ibid., 248.

15. Department of the Treasury, "Lessons Learned from the Privatization of Sallie Mae," 24.

16. As one of the largest financial scandals in the history of the United States, the Savings and Loan Crisis emerged in the late 1970s and came to a head in the 1980s, finally ending in the early 1990s. In an atmosphere of volatile interest rates spilling over from the 1970s into the 1980s, large numbers of depositors removed their funds from savings and loan institutions (S&Ls) and put them in money market funds, where they could charge higher interest rates where they were not as heavily regulated with interest rate caps. As S&L regulations loosened over time in order to combat the wave of transfers to money market funds, S&Ls engaged in progressively risky activities, including commercial real estate lending and investments in junk bonds.

17. CBO, *Controlling the Risks of Government-Sponsored Enterprises*, 262–65.

18. Department of the Treasury, "Lessons Learned from the Privatization of Sallie Mae," 7.

19. GAO, "GSE Report," May 1991, 32; letter dated March 7, 1991, from Timothy G. Greene, EVP and general counsel of SLMA, to Jill K. Ouseley, director, Division of Market Finance, Department of the Treasury.

20. Department of the Treasury, "Lessons Learned from the Privatization of Sallie Mae," 7.

21. Stanton, "The Privatization of Sallie Mae and Its Consequences," 15.

22. Department of the Treasury, "Lessons Learned from the Privatization of Sallie Mae," 20.

23. Ibid., 21.

24. Ibid.

25. Ibid.

26. Department of the Treasury, "Lessons Learned from the Privatization of Sallie Mae," 22.

27. David Kleinbard, "Direct Student Loans Would Save Government $4.7 Billion, GAO Says," *Bloomberg News*, November 25, 1992, retrieved from Department of the Treasury, "Lessons Learned from the Privatization of Sallie Mae," 21.

28. Department of the Treasury, "Lessons Learned from the Privatization of Sallie Mae," 22.

29. Subcommittee on Education, Arts and Humanities, Committee on Labor and Human Resources, U.S. Senate, *Privatization of Sallie Mae and Connie Lee*, hearing, June 20, 1995, 12 (testimony of Lawrence A. Hough, president and CEO, Sallie Mae), 4, retrieved from Stanton, "The Privatization of Sallie Mae and Its Consequences," 16.

30. Ibid.

31. Department of the Treasury, "Lessons Learned from the Privatization of Sallie Mae," 22.

32. Ibid., 27.

33. Sallie Mae, *The Restructuring of Sallie Mae*, 13–14, retrieved from Stanton, "The Privatization of Sallie Mae and Its Consequences," 17.

34. Title VI of Pub. L. No. 104-208, enacted September 30, 1996. 20 U.S.C. Sec. 1087-3, 12 U.S.C. Sec. 1828(s) and 12 U.S.C. Sec. 1781(e).

35. Department of the Treasury, "Lessons Learned from the Privatization of Sallie Mae," 35.

36. "In 1982, AT&T and the Department of Justice settled the antitrust case against AT&T. AT&T agreed to break itself up into several firms in 1984. One firm, AT&T, provided long-distance service, and seven other firms ('Baby Bells') provided local telephone service in different regions. The Department of Justice apparently felt that a vertically integrated telephone company, one that provided local and long-distance service, was not required for productive efficiency, or that there were other offsetting gains from the divestiture.

According to the Department of Justice, the vertical structure of the company provided an opportunity for unfair competition against other providers of long-distance service. For example, by charging high local rates or by providing poor local service to other providers of long-distance service (which require local service), AT&T could harm long-distance competitors. Another concern of the Department of Justice was the difficulty of monitoring cost-shifting among AT&T's regulated (telephone) and other relatively unregulated businesses (such as the manufacture of telephones and other equipment). The resulting breakup of the telephone company presumably mitigated the government's concerns." Dennis W. Carlton and Jeffrey M. Perloff, *Modern Industrial Organization* (Boston: Pearson/Addison Wesley, 2005), "The Breakup of AT&T" (online resource), http://wps.aw.com/aw_carltonper_modernio_4/21/5566/1425000.cw/content/index.html (accessed May 2, 2016).

37. Sallie Mae Internal Memorandum to file, Sallie Mae/AT&T Comparison, from Timothy G. Greene, EVP and general counsel, June 9, 1994; Department of the Treasury, "Lessons Learned from the Privatization of Sallie Mae," 36.

38. Testimony of Leo Kornfeld, senior advisor to the secretary of education, before the House Joint Hearing, May 3, 1995, retrieved from Department of the Treasury, "Lessons Learned from the Privatization of Sallie Mae," 40–41.

39. Department of the Treasury, "Lessons Learned from the Privatization of Sallie Mae," 36.

40. Stanton, "The Privatization of Sallie Mae and Its Consequences," p. 21, figure 5: "The Mechanics of Removing Government Sponsorship."

41. Department of the Treasury, "Lessons Learned from the Privatization of Sallie Mae," 37.

42. Ibid.

43. H.R. 1617, Consolidated and Reformed Education, Employment, and Rehabilitation Systems Act (CAREERS Act), introduced May 11, 1995, retrieved from Department of the Treasury, "Lessons Learned from the Privatization of Sallie Mae," 43–44.

44. Ibid. The proposal was made by the chair of the Senate Budget Committee, Pete Domenici.

45. Testimony of Darcy Bradbury, deputy assistant secretary of the treasury, before the Senate Subcommittee on Education, Arts, and Humanities of the Committee on Labor and Human Resources, June 20, 1995, see appendix 4 to this report, retrieved from Department of the Treasury, "Lessons Learned from the Privatization of Sallie Mae," 47.

46. The House approved of H.R. 1720, the portion of the Careers Bill that had to do with SLMA's privatization, on September 24, 1996, but the Senate did not act on that bill. It came up once again as part of H.R. 3610, the 1997 Omnibus Budget Reconciliation Act.

47. Department of the Treasury, "Lessons Learned from the Privatization of Sallie Mae," 47.

48. Ibid.

49. Ibid., 49.

50. Ibid.

51. Ibid.

52. Ibid.

53. Higher Education Act of 1965, Reorganization of the Student Loan Marketing Association through the Formation of a Holding Company, Sec. 440(2)(a)(3), 441.

54. Department of the Treasury, "Lessons Learned from the Privatization of Sallie Mae," 49.

55. Higher Education Act of 1965, Sec. 440(3), 447.

56. Ibid., Sec. 440(c)(1), 440. More specifically, the law dictated that: (1) GSE funds and assets be kept and accounted for separately and be used only for GSE purposes, (2) the GSE keep a headquarters physically separate from the private company, (3) no presidential-appointee director of the GSE could serve on the holding company's board of directors, (4) one officer of the GSE had to be solely an officer of the GSE, (5) transactions between the GSE and its private-sector affiliates be conducted as arm's-length transactions, (6) the GSE was prohibited from extending credit to the private-sector affiliates, and (7) any GSE funds collected by the holding company on behalf of the GSE had to be immediately deposited into a GSE-controlled account. The law also prevented the holding company from transferring its ownership of the GSE's shares or causing the GSE to be liquidated or put into bankruptcy without the approval of the Treasury and the Department of Education.

57. Testimony of Darcy Bradbury, deputy assistant secretary of the treasury, before the Senate Subcommittee on Education, Arts, and Humanities of the Committee on Labor and Human Resources, June 20, 1995, see appendix 4 to this report, retrieved from Department of the Treasury, "Lessons Learned from the Privatization of Sallie Mae," 47.

58. Higher Education Act of 1965, Sec. 440(8)(a), 442–43.

59. Department of the Treasury, "Lessons Learned from the Privatization of Sallie Mae," 51.

60. Ibid.

61. Ibid.

62. Ibid.

63. Stanton, "The Privatization of Sallie Mae and Its Consequences," p. 20, figure 5: "The Mechanics of Removing Government Sponsorship."

64. 20 U.S.C. § 1087-2 (c)(1), retrieved from Department of the Treasury, "Lessons Learned from the Privatization of Sallie Mae," 53.

65. Department of the Treasury, "Lessons Learned from the Privatization of Sallie Mae," 53.

66. Ibid.

67. Ibid.

68. Ibid., 54.

69. Ibid.

70. Ibid.

71. SLMA board of director minutes for meeting held January 24, 1997, 52, retrieved from Department of the Treasury, "Lessons Learned from the Privatization of Sallie Mae," 54.

72. Ibid.

73. Ibid.

6. RIGGED

1. USA Education, Inc. (formerly SLM Holding Corporation), Form 10-K for the Fiscal Year ended December 31, 2000, 4, retrieved from Thomas H. Stanton, "The Privatization of Sallie Mae and Its Consequences," p. 22, figure 6: "Sallie Mae's Growth Student Loans Held and Securitized 1997–2006."

2. Stanton, "The Privatization of Sallie Mae and Its Consequences," 22.

3. Ibid., 23.

4. Suzanne Mettler, *Degrees of Inequality: How the Politics of Higher Education Sabotaged the American Dream* (New York: Basic Books, 2014), 137.

5. Stephen Burd, "Student Loan Companies Under Scrutiny for Incentives to Colleges," *Chronicle of Higher Education*, October 17, 2003; Megan Bar-

nett, Julian E. Barnes, and Danielle Knight, "Big Money on Campus; In the Multibillion Dollar World of Student Loans, Big Lenders Are Finding New Ways to Drain Uncle Sam's Coffers," *U.S. News & World Report*, October 27, 2003, retrieved from Stanton, "The Privatization of Sallie Mae and Its Consequences," 23.

6. Ibid.

7. Department of the Treasury, "Lessons Learned from the Privatization of Sallie Mae," 70.

8. Ibid.

9. Lindsay Renick Mayer, "Sallie Mae Finds Friends as Major Student Loan Bill Moves through Congress," September 23, 2009, www.opensecrets .org/news/2009/09/sallie-mae-finds-friends-as-ma.html (accessed January 20, 2014).

10. Higher Education Amendments of 1998, sponsored by Rep. Howard McKeon (CA-25), H.R. 105-244, http://thomas.loc.gov/cgi-bin/bdquery/ z?d105:H.R.6 (accessed January 20, 2014).

11. Jean Braucher, *Mortgaging Human Capital: Federally Funded Subprime Higher Education* (Lexington, VA: Washington and Lee University, 2012), 27.

12. Supra at p. 80.

13. Center for Responsive Politics, "SLM Corp. Contributions and Lobbying Expenditures," www.opensecrets.org/orgs/summary.php?id= D000022253&cycle=A (accessed January 20, 2014).

14. Braucher, *Mortgaging Human Capital*, 27–28.

15. Thomas H. Jackson, *The Logic and Limits of Bankruptcy Law* (Cambridge: Harvard University Press, 1986), 248–49.

16. Stanton, "The Privatization of Sallie Mae and Its Consequences," 26.

17. Ibid.

18. Stephen Burd, "Should Borrowers Fear a Student-Loan Behemoth? Sallie Mae's Massive Growth May Reshape the Loan Industry," *Chronicle of Higher Education*, August 11, 2000, retrieved from Stanton, "The Privatization of Sallie Mae and Its Consequences, 26.

19. Stanton, "The Privatization of Sallie Mae and Its Consequences," 26.

20. Ibid.

21. Matthew Quirk, "The Best Class Money Can Buy," *Atlantic Monthly*, November 2005. This technique has effectively changed financial aid from a method to help low-income students to a tool that attracts high-scoring students through data mining and price techniques that originated in the airline and marketing industries. Retrieved from Stanton, "The Privatization of Sallie Mae and Its Consequences," 27.

22. Stanton, "The Privatization of Sallie Mae and Its Consequences," 27.

23. USA Education, Inc. (formerly SLM Holding Corporation), Form 10-K for the Fiscal Year ended December 31, 2000, 7–8, retrieved from Stanton, "The Privatization of Sallie Mae and Its Consequences," 26.

24. Stanton, "The Privatization of Sallie Mae and Its Consequences," 27.

25. SLM Corporation, Form 10-K for the Fiscal Year ended December 31, 2003, 9, retrieved from Stanton, "The Privatization of Sallie Mae and Its Consequences," 27.

26. Ibid.

27. Stanton, "The Privatization of Sallie Mae and Its Consequences," 28.

28. SLM Corporation, Form 10-K for the Fiscal Year ended December 31, 2004, 9, retrieved from Stanton, "The Privatization of Sallie Mae and Its Consequences," 28.

29. Common Equity is the amount that all common shareholders have invested in a company, including the value of the common shares themselves, retained earnings, and additional paid-in capital.

30. Sallie Mae Annual Forms 10K, 1996-2004, retrieved from Stanton, "The Privatization of Sallie Mae and Its Consequences," 28.

31. Stanton, "The Privatization of Sallie Mae and Its Consequences," p. 31, figure 11: "Sallie Mae Corporate Structure."

32. Ibid., 32.

33. Ibid.

34. Ibid.

35. The Federal Home Loan Bank (FHLB) is split into twelve U.S. government-sponsored banking districts that provide funding and liquidity to American financial institutions for home mortgage loans, small business, rural, agricultural, and economic development lending. The FHLB was chartered by Congress under the Federal Home Loan Bank Act of 1932, with the mission of providing member financial institutions with financial products and services that assist and enhance the financing of housing and community lending.

36. Sallie Mae, "Choose the Smart Option Student Loans," www.salliemae.com/landing/sosl_int_DirectPlus, retrieved from a letter to FHFA acting director Edward DeMarco from Elizabeth Warren, June 24, 2013.

37. Ibid.

38. Senate Banking, Housing and Urban Affairs Committee, Private Student Loans Hearing, Testimony by Rohit Chopra, assistant director and student loan ombudsman consumer financial protection, June 25, 2013, www.youtube.com/watch?v=2pDqsutEaxk (accessed January 22, 2014).

39. U.S. Census Bureau, "Income, Poverty and Health Insurance in the United States," P60-239 (2011), retrieved from *Student Loan Affordability: Analysis of Public Input on Impact and Solution* (Washington DC: Consumer Financial Protection Bureau, 2013).

40. John Hechinger and Janet Lorin, "Sallie Mae Split Marks Bet on Abused Private Student Loans," *Bloomberg*, May 31, 2013, www.bloomberg.com/news/2013-05-31/sallie-mae-split-marks-bet-on-much-abused-private-student-loans.html (accessed January 12, 2014).

41. Halah Touryalai, "What Sallie Mae's Split Says about Student Loans," *Forbes*, May 29, 2013, www.forbes.com/sites/halahtouryalai/2013/05/29/what-sallie-maes-split-says-about-student-loans (accessed January 12, 2014).

42. Burke&Quick Partners, "Sallie Mae and the Student Loan Market," table 1: "Asset Breakdown," July 24, 2013. www.bqpartners.com/sites/bqp/files/attachments/Sallie%20Mae%20and%20the%20Student%20Loan%20Market.pdf (accessed March 31, 2014).

43. Ibid.

44. Hechinger and Lorin, "Sallie Mae Split Marks Bet on Abused Private Student Loans."

45. Sarah Mulholland, "Sallie Mae to Split into Two Companies as Remondi Named CEO," *Bloomberg*, May 29, 2013, www.bloomberg.com/news/2013-05-29/sallie-mae-to-split-into-two-companies-as-jack-remondi-named-ceo.html (accessed January 12, 2014).

46. Multiples reflect the market's perceptions of a company's growth prospects, so two companies with similar prospects and operating characteristics should trade at similar multiples.

47. Ruth Simon and Saabira Chaudhuri, "Sallie Mae to Separate Banking Unit," *Wall Street Journal*, May 29, 2013, http://online.wsj.com/news/articles/SB10001424127887324866904578512864250143212 (accessed January 12, 2014).

48. Hechinger and Lorin, "Sallie Mae Split Marks Bet on Abused Private Student Loans."

49. Mulholland, "Sallie Mae to Split into Two Companies as Remondi Named CEO."

50. Halah Touryalai, "Sallie Mae Reports a Pop in Private Student Loans, Bets College Costs Will Rise," *Forbes*, October 16, 2013, www.forbes.com/sites/halahtouryalai/2013/10/16/sallie-mae-reports-a-pop-in-private-student-loans-bets-college-costs-will-rise (accessed January 12, 2014).

51. Sallie Mae Shareholder Information, "Stock Chart: Historical Price Lookup," 2014, www.salliemae.com/about/investors/stockholderinfo/stockcharts/historical-price-lookup/default.aspx (accessed January 25, 2014).

52. Rohit Chopra, "Annual Report of the CFPB Student Loan Ombudsman," CFPB, October 16, 2013, 4.

53. Chopra, "Annual Report of the CFPB Student Loan Ombudsman," table 2: "Private Student Loan Complaints by Company, October 2012–September 2013," 7.

54. Ibid.

55. Chopra, "Annual Report of the CFPB Student Loan Ombudsman," 8.

56. Ibid.

57. Ibid., 9.

58. Ibid.

59. Ibid., 10.

60. Ibid.

61. Ibid., 11.

62. Ibid.

63. Ibid.

64. Ibid.

65. Ibid., 14.

66. Lisa Noller, "Regulatory: Sallie Mae Case Lowers Rule 9(b) Standards," *Inside Counsel*, February 22, 2012, www.insidecounsel.com/2012/02/22/regulatory-sallie-mae-case-lowers-rule-9b-standard (accessed December 29, 2013).

67. Ibid.

68. Shahien Nasiripour, "Sallie Mae, Education Department Under Fire for Student Loans to Military Service Members," *Huffington Post*, August 8, 2013, www.huffingtonpost.com/2013/08/08/sallie-mae-education-military_n _3729092.html (accessed December 29, 2013).

69. Chopra, "Annual Report of the CFPB Student Loan Ombudsman," 7.

70. Senate Banking, Housing and Urban Affairs Committee, Private Student Loans Hearing, testimony by Rohit Chopra, assistant director and student loan ombudsman consumer financial protection, June 25, 2013, 3, www.consumerfinance.gov/newsroom/the-cfpb-before-the-senate-committee-on-banking-housing-and-urban-affairs (accessed January 25, 2014).

7. BREAKING BACKS TO BALANCE BUDGETS

1. FinAid, *Direct Loans vs. the FFEL Program*, 2014, www.finaid.org/loans/dl-vs-ffel.phtml (accessed February 2, 2014).

2. Thomas H. Stanton, "The Privatization of Sallie Mae and Its Consequences," 25.

3. Ibid., 15.

4. Informal term for any attempt to block or delay Senate action on a bill or other matter by debating it at length, by offering numerous procedural motions, or by any other delaying or obstructive actions. In order to override a filibuster, sixty votes are needed to bring cloture and end debate. Retrieved from the U.S. Senate, Glossary, www.senate.gov/reference/glossary_term/

filibuster.htm (accessed February 2, 2014).

5. FinAid, "Student Aid and Fiscal Responsibility Act of 2009," 2014, www.finaid.org/educators/20090715hr3221.phtml (accessed February 2, 2014).

6. Health Care and Education Reconciliation Act of 2010, H.R. 4872, Sec. 2201, 1074, www.govtrack.us/congress/bills/111/hr4872/text (accessed January 12, 2014).

7. Ibid., Sec. 2101(C), 1074.

8. Ibid., Sec. 2103, 1074.

9. Ibid., Sec. 2213, 1074.

10. Health Care and Education Reconciliation Act of 2010, H.R. 4872, Sec. 2102, 1074, www.govtrack.us/congress/bills/111/hr4872/text (accessed January 12, 2014).

11. The White House, "The Health Care and Education Reconciliation Act," 2014, www.whitehouse.gov/issues/education/higher-education/making-college-affordable (accessed January 12, 2014).

12. Federal Student Aid, "Direct Subsidized and Unsubsidized Loans," U.S. Department of Education, 2014, http://studentaid.ed.gov/types/loans/subsidized-unsubsidized#what%27s-the-difference (accessed February 8, 2014).

13. Ibid.

14. Deferment is a postponement of payment on a loan that is allowed under certain conditions and during which interest does not accrue on Direct Subsidized Loans, Subsidized Federal Stafford Loans, and Federal Perkins Loans. All other federal student loans that are deferred will continue to accrue interest. Any unpaid interest that accrued during the deferment period may be added to the principal balance (capitalized) of the loan(s). Retrieved from Federal Student Aid, *Glossary*, U.S. Department of Education, 2014, http://studentaid.ed.gov/glossary#Deferment.

15. Forbearance is a period during which your monthly loan payments are temporarily suspended or reduced. Your lender may grant you a forbearance if you are willing but unable to make loan payments due to certain types of financial hardships. During forbearance, principal payments are postponed but interest continues to accrue. Unpaid interest that accrues during the forbearance will be added to the principal balance (capitalized) of your loan(s), increasing the total amount you owe. Retrieved from Federal Student Aid, Glossary, U.S. Department of Education, 2014, http://studentaid.ed.gov/glossary#Forbearance.

16. Ibid.

17. Ibid.

18. Federal Student Aid, "Interest Rates and Fees," U.S. Department of Education, 2014, http://studentaid.ed.gov/types/loans/interest-rates (accessed February 8, 2014).

19. Federal Student Aid, "Direct Subsidized and Unsubsidized Loans," U.S. Department of Education, 2014, http://studentaid.ed.gov/types/loans/subsidized-unsubsidized#what%27s-the-difference (accessed February 8, 2014)

20. Ibid.

21. Ibid.

22. Federal Student Aid, "Direct PLUS Loans," U.S. Department of Education, 2014, http://studentaid.ed.gov/types/loans/plus (accessed February 8, 2014).

23. Ibid.

24. Federal Student Aid, "Federal Perkins Loans," U.S. Department of Education, 2014, http://studentaid.ed.gov/types/loans/perkins (accessed February 8, 2014).

25. Ibid.

26. Ibid.

27. Federal Student Aid, "Repayment Plans," U.S. Department of Education, 2014, http://studentaid.ed.gov/repay-loans/understand/plans (accessed February 8, 2014).

28. Ibid.

29. Ibid.

30. Consolidation is the process of combining one or more loans into a single new loan. Retrieved from Federal Student Aid, Glossary, U.S. Department of Education, 2014, http://studentaid.ed.gov/glossary#Consolidation.

31. Discretionary income accounts for your income minus the poverty guidelines for your family size. Retrieved from Federal Student Aid, Glossary, U.S. Department of Education, 2014, http://studentaid.ed.gov/glossary#Discretionary_Income (accessed February 8, 2014).

32. Federal Student Aid, "Repayment Plans," U.S. Department of Education, 2014, http://studentaid.ed.gov/repay-loans/understand/plans (accessed February 8, 2014).

33. Ibid.

34. Ibid.

35. Ibid.

36. Ibid.

37. Ibid.

38. Borrowers will make payments to their lender, the organization that made the loan initially. The lender could be a bank, credit union, or other lending institution. The lender will provide borrowers with information about

their repayment terms and start date. Retrieved from Federal Student Aid, "Repayment Plans," U.S. Department of Education, 2014, http://studentaid.ed.gov/repay-loans/understand/plans (accessed February 8, 2014).

39. College Cost Reduction and Access Act, H.R. 2669, Sec. 201(b), 8, www.govtrack.us/congress/bills/110/hr2669 (accessed February 8, 2014)

40. Bipartisan Student Loan Certainty Act of 2013, H.R. 1911, Sec. 2(8)(A), 1, www.govtrack.us/congress/bills/113/hr1911/text (accessed February 9, 2014).

41. MyBankTracker, "How Treasury Yields Affect Student Loan Rates under New Bill," *Huffington Post*, August 16, 2013, www.huffingtonpost.com/mybanktracker/how-treasury-yields-affec_b_3762786.html?utm_hp _ref=college (accessed February 2, 2014).

42. GL Advisor, "Dissecting the Bipartisan Student Loan Certainty Act of 2013," Graduate Leverage Insurance Services, 2012, www.gladvisor.com/bipartisan-student-loan-certainty-act-of-2013.aspx (accessed February 2, 2014).

43. Jonathan Weisman, "Cost Estimate Puts in Doubt Deal Covering Student Loans," *New York Times*, July 11, 2013, www.nytimes.com/2013/07/12/us/politics/tentative-senate-deal-reached-on-student-loan-rates.html?_r=0 (accessed February 9, 2014).

44. Josh Mitchell, "Senate Backs Student-Loan Bill," *Wall Street Journal*, July 24, 2013, http://online.wsj.com/news/articles/SB100014241278 87323971204578626420131976286 (accessed February 9, 2014).

45. Kathryn Baron, "Dems Argue over Bill to Reduce Student Loan Rates," *EdSource Today*, July 23, 2013, www.google.com/url?sa=t&rct=j&q=&esrc =s&frm=1&source=web&cd=1&ved=0CCcQFjAA&url=http%3A %2F%2Fedsource.org%2Ftoday%2F2013%2Fdems-argue-over-bill-to -reduce-student-loan-rates%2F36477&ei=VFj4UqGOJ8mwyQGwx4CwBA &usg=AFQjCNEfN4m3APN0SjHDjNc83NqVTeDsfQ&sig2 =gRybreughSR3hFeqOm8bBQ (accessed February 9, 2014).

46. Josh Mitchell, "Senate Backs Student-Loan Bill," *Wall Street Journal*, July 24, 2013, http://online.wsj.com/news/articles/SB100014241278 87323971204578626420131976286 (accessed February 9, 2014).

47. Federal Student Aid, "Federal versus Private Loans, U.S. Department of Education," 2014, http://studentaid.ed.gov/types/loans/federal-vs-private (accessed February 8, 2014).

48. CBO May 2013 Baseline Projections for the Student Loan Program, table 1, 2013, retrieved from Glenn Kessler, "Elizabeth Warren's Claim That the U.S. Earns $51 Billion in Profits on Student Loans," *Washington Post*, July 11, 2013, www.washingtonpost.com/blogs/fact-checker/post/elizabeth-warrens-claim-that-the-us-earns-51-billion-in-profits-on-student-loans/2013/07/10/

7769a3c2-e9b8-11e2-aa9f-c03a72e2d342_blog.html (accessed January 4, 2014).

49. Senator Elizabeth Warren, "Senator Warren Introduces Legislation Extending to Students Same Interest Rates Enjoyed By Big Banks," remarks by Senator Elizabeth Warren on student loan interest rates as prepared for delivery, May 8, 2013, www.warren.senate.gov/?p=press_release&id=81 (accessed February 9, 2014).

50. Kayla Webley, "Elizabeth Warren: Students Should Get the Same Rate as the Bankers," *Time Business and Money*, May 10, 2013, http://business.time.com/2013/05/10/elizabeth-warren-students-should-get-the-same-rate-as-the-bankers (accessed February 2, 2014).

51. Bank on Students Loan Fairness Act, S. 897, Sec. 3(E), 3, www.govtrack.us/congress/bills/113/s897 (accessed February 2, 2014).

52. Supra at p. 168.

53. Ibid., 128.

54. National Defense Education Act, Title I: General Provisions, Sec. 101, September 2, 1958, 1581.

55. Jonathan Z. Zhou, "The Warren Bubble Act," *Harvard Crimson*, May 15, 2013, www.thecrimson.com/column/homo-economicus/article/2013/5/15/warren-bubble-harvard (accessed February 2, 2014).

56. FinAid, "Student Loan Bankruptcy Exception," U.S. Bankruptcy Code in 1978 (11 USC 101 et seq, P.L. 95-598, §523[a][8], 1978), www.finaid.org/questions/bankruptcyexception.phtml (accessed February 2, 2013).

57. Ibid., 166.

8. A STAKE IN THE GAME

1. Anthony P. Carnevale and Ban Cheah, *Hard Times: College Majors, Unemployment, and Earnings: Not All Degrees Are Created Equal* (Washington DC: Georgetown University Center on Education and the Workforce, 2012), 3. https://cew.georgetown.edu/wp-content/uploads/2014/11/Unemployment.Final_.update1.pdf (accessed February 2, 2014).

2. Ibid., 5.

3. Ibid.

4. Angela Johnson, "Business Majors Most Likely to Be Underemployed, Report Finds," *CNN Money*, June 19, 2013, http://money.cnn.com/2013/06/19/pf/college/underemployed (accessed February 2, 2014).

5. "College Scorecard," White House, College Affordability and Transparency Center, www.whitehouse.gov/issues/education/higher-education/college-score-card (accessed January 22, 2014).

6. *The Higher Education Opportunity Act*, P.L. 110-315, Sec. 120, 41, August 14, 2008, retrieved from the Department of Education, www2.ed.gov/policy/highered/leg/hea08/index.html (accessed January 22, 2014).

7. "College Scorecard," Department of Education, College Affordability and Transparency Center, http://collegecost.ed.gov/scorecard (accessed January 22, 2014).

8. Federal Student Aid, "Annual Report FY 2014," U.S. Department of Education, November 14, 2014, 7, www2.ed.gov/about/reports/annual/2014report/fsa-report.pdf (accessed January 7, 2016).

9. Supra at p. 148.

10. "Employment by Major Industry Sector," Bureau of Labor Statistics, U.S. Department of Labor, www.bls.gov/emp/ep_table_201.htm (accessed January 24, 2014).

11. William Patrick Leonard, "A New Model for Containing College Costs: The Lean College," Rio Grande Foundation, November 4, 2013, 2, www.riograndefoundation.org/downloads/rgf_college_costs.pdf (accessed January 24, 2014).

12. Chester Finn, "Why Must College Be So Costly," *Hoover Institution News*, March 8, 2004, www.hoover.org/news/daily-report/24885 (accessed January 22, 2014).

13. Leonard, "A New Model for Containing College Costs," 7.

14. "College Assistance Plan," CAP Advisory Services Inc., www.collegeassistanceplan.com/plan.

9. THE *NEW* AMERICAN COLLEGE AND UNIVERSITY

1. National Center for Education Statistics, Educational Institutions, Institute of Education Sciences, U.S. Department of Education, https://nces.ed.gov/fastfacts/display.asp?id=84 (accessed January 5, 2016).

2. Frederick Rudolph and John R. Thelin, *The American College and University: A History* (Athens: University of Georgia Press, 1990), 238.

3. Ibid., 133.

4. "Original Papers in Relation to a Course of Liberal Education," *The American Journal of Science and Arts* 15 (1829): 297–351.

5. Anthony P. Carnevale and Ban Cheah, *Hard Times: College Majors, Unemployment, and Earnings: Not All Degrees Are Created Equal* (Washington DC: Georgetown University Center on Education and the Workforce, 2012), 14.

6. Federal Student Aid, *Annual Report FY 2014*, U.S. Department of Education, November 14, 2014, 7, www2.ed.gov/about/reports/annual/2014report/fsa-report.pdf (accessed January 7, 2016).

7. Rudolph, *The American College and University*, 238.

8. Adam Smith, *An Inquiry into the Nature and Causes of the Wealth of Nations* (London: W. Strahan and T. Cadell, 1776), 8.

9. Ibid., 10.

10. Ibid., 11.

11. Jon Marcus, "The Unexpected Schools Championing the Liberal Arts," *The Atlantic*, October 15, 2015, www.theatlantic.com/education/archive/2015/10/the-unexpected-schools-championing-the-liberal-arts/410500 (accessed January 7, 2016).

12. Ibid.

13. Ibid.

14. Ibid.

15. Beau Willimon, *House of Cards*, S3: E7, "Chapter 33," Netflix, 2015.

16. Christine Sarikas, "SAT/ACT Prep Online Guides and Tips: Complete List of High School Electives," PrepScholar, August 15, 2015, http://blog.prepscholar.com/complete-list-of-high-school-electives (accessed January 31, 2016).

17. Cecile Hoareau McGrath, Marie Louise Henham, Anne Corbett, Niccolo Durazzi, Michael Frearson, Barbara Janta, Bregtje W. Kamphuis, Eriko Katashiro, Nina Brankovic, Benoit Guerin, Catriona Manville, Inga Schwartz, and Daniel Schweppenstedde, *Higher Education Entrance Qualifications and Exams in Europe: A Comparison* (Brussels: European Parliament, 2014), 31.

18. Tamara Berger-Proßdorf, "Educational Systems in Europe," *The Montana Professor* 6, no. 1 (Winter 1996), http://mtprof.msun.edu/Win1996/TamaraBP.html (accessed January 31, 2016).

19. Ibid.

20. Ibid.

21. Ibid.

22. Ibid.

23. Motoko Rich, "As Graduation Rates Rise, Experts Fear Diplomas Come Up Short," *New York Times*, December 26, 2015, www.nytimes.com/2015/12/27/us/as-graduation-rates-rise-experts-fear-standards-have-fallen.html?emc=eta1&_r=0 (accessed January 29, 2016).

24. Editorial Board, "The Counterfeit High School Diploma," *New York Times*, December 31, 2015, www.nytimes.com/2015/12/31/opinion/the-counterfeit-high-school-diploma.html?emc=eta1 (accessed January 10, 2016).

25. *Patch Adams*, Dir. Tom Shadyac, Blue Wolf Productions, 1998. Film.

26. John Adams, "Argument in Defense of the British Soldiers in the Boston Massacre Trials," December 4, 1770.

27. Jillian Berman, "Watch America's Student-Loan Debt Grow $2,726 Every Second," *Market Watch*, January 30, 2016, www.marketwatch.com/story/every-second-americans-get-buried-under-another-3055-in-student-loan-debt-2015-06-10 (accessed January 31, 2016).

28. "IMF World Economic Outlook (WEO)," October 2015, http://knoema.com/nwnfkne/world-gdp-ranking-2015-data-and-charts (accessed January 30, 2016).

29. Allen Oscar Hansen, *Liberalism and American Education in the Eighteenth Century* (New York: Macmillan, 1926), 52–53.

30. Ibid., 22.

31. Samuel Eliot Morison, *Harvard College in the Seventeenth Century* (Cambridge: Harvard University Press, 1936), 433.

ABOUT THE AUTHOR

Kevin W. Connell is a native resident of Rochester, New York, where he earned a BA in political science from the University of Rochester. After graduating *cum laude* and Phi Beta Kappa from the University of Rochester in 2015, Kevin now attends William & Mary Law School, where he is expected to graduate in 2018 with the intent to practice law and enter politics.